DEDICATION

To my parents Wesley and Sari and parents in law Errol and Pam who mentored me in their own way, and my many other mentors who have helped me through my journey in life.

To my darling wife and partner Robyn, and sons Josh and Sam, who have supported me and kept me grounded to ensure my continual relevance to them and those around us.

First published in 2020 by Garry Browne

A catalogue entry for this book is available from the National Library of Australia.

ISBN: 978-1-925921-81-6

Printed in Australia by McPherson's Printing
Project management, cover design and interior design by
Michael Hanrahan Publishing

The paper this book is printed on is certified as environmentally friendly.

Disclaimer

Contents

Branding – but not as you know it

The content of this book is perhaps not what you are expecting. It's about branding – but not as most people know it. It focuses on *personal* branding rather than product or service branding, although many of the intrinsic elements of what makes a good product or service brand – such as Qantas, McDonald's, Tabasco, Christian Dior, Chanel, Burberry, Apple – apply to you as a personal brand as well.

EVERYONE IS A BRAND

I have always had a passion for trademarks and brands, whoever or whatever they were or are today. When I first thought of writing this book I was working on several projects that were more related to community and humanitarian brands than business or personal branding. It intrigues me that our lives consist of so many brands and yet people generally do not recognise this in relation to their own lives and their values.

I believe everyone is a brand of some description.

Most cultures define people as being individuals, as someone special and unique. However, we rarely think of people as being a brand (although that's changed somewhat over the past 10 years), but we will describe someone who does not know what they want or who they are as being 'lost' or 'stranded'.

Consumer brands are the basis by which we make so many decisions in life. They are the standard by which we choose so many things in life. At the personal level someone's brand is how others describe, know, interact, respect and follow them. To be a successful, trusted brand – consumer or individual – is to have reached a high standard. This standard, or brand recognition, is based on a set of actual and perceived expectations. People who have a 'leadership brand' have set themselves apart from the crowd and they are respected and followed. As such they can set and progress their agenda, have influence and impact. They are successfully creating 'brand you'.

Growing up I really didn't know what branding meant, but I did know what it was like to be left out, ignored or forgotten. I was a nobody in my mind. Looking back I realise that I didn't have a brand (a way to stand out from the crowd) by which everyone could define me. I was surrounded by intelligent classmates and athletic stars who excelled in rugby or basketball. These boys were defined by either their brains or sporting prowess; they were branded stars.

I hated feeling like I was stranded, but was smart enough to know I needed to carve out a position where others could not go or where the barriers to entry were low if I was going to change this. Long-distance running was something that most of the other boys didn't participate in – they didn't have the patience or persistence – so I picked this. I was willing to take the appropriate course of action to build my brand.

In *Brand New Brand You* I share my over 40 years of experience in FMCG (fast-moving consumer goods) and in the not-for-profit sector to help people and businesses look at the world in a different way and encourage a branded approach to life. Among other benefits, understanding the dynamics of building and maintaining a strong, positive personal brand can build self-esteem in those who don't have it, and develop those who have self-esteem to craft and create a better positioning for themselves in personal and business life.

YOUR BRAND VALUES

Talking about the value of 'brand you' and where the benefits lie in actively managing your brand from quite a young age, I am not talking about the value in monetary terms but in terms of your values. Your values go to the core of who 'brand you' is.

We all live our lives on a basis of values and ideals. They take years to develop and craft, and in many cases we unconsciously absorb some or most of our values from our immediate family and close peer groups. The combination and expression of your values on a consistent basis becomes your brand whether you actively manage it or not.

The external description for your values is what I call 'reputation'. Or, as Jeff Bezos said, 'Your brand is what other people say about you when you're not in the room.'

Another definition I like is that your reputation is the difference between what you say and what you do.

Reputations are always filtered through the sentiments, prejudices and interests of others which, in turn, influences how we see ourselves.

Labels, nicknames and tags – these are not ways of branding, they are descriptors that others place on you as terms of endearment and affection as opposed to what you stand for. If you are conscious of your brand and what you want to stand for then you must be in control and not leave it to others to determine.

YOUR REPUTATION IS EVERYTHING

Our brand and what and how we wish to be seen and positioned must be a creation of our own doing. It is built up over your lifetime, and can take just a moment or two to lose. Our reputation is everything, and for me I guard it jealously. You too should be thinking about what it means to have a brand and reputation and how quickly and easily you can lose them.

A critical aspect of your brand is relevance, relevance from the day you are born to the day you die. As such, it's a journey throughout your life and across different aspects of your life. If you don't find and then maintain relevance you'll become stranded all through your life or at different times in your life.

Just like your reputation, your relevance requires active management.

And reputation doesn't necessarily translate to relevance, nor does recognition.

Today we see the outcome of the first generation of people who have grasped the responsibility of curating what others think about them. Just look at Beyoncé, Jay Z, Taylor Swift, the Kardashians, the Royal Family, Freddy Mercury and his estate, Mick Jagger and the Rolling Stones, Roger Federer and others.

YOU HAVE ONE WHETHER YOU MANAGE IT OR NOT

Brand New Brand You is about exploring the intersection between reputation, recognition and relevance. No one can opt out of having a reputation; you have one whether you manage it or not. Some people are recognised but have no relevance, others have a reputation and are not relevant.

So how do you remain relevant throughout your life and develop a strong, valued and respected reputation? And why should you care? These and other questions around personal branding are what we're exploring in this book.

If you want to make an impact on your community, business or the world, you need to be relevant and have a reputation that will support the messages and initiatives you want to focus on. Your values, not your value, is what drives this.

At the time of writing, the COVID-19 pandemic is a complete game changer for the way businesses operate both through the pandemic itself and afterwards. And perhaps it's the wake-up call we all needed. The reset from a focus on what's in it for me rather than what's best for our community. A reset from our smugness and sense of complacency and entitlement to a more caring, more supportive, nurturing and gentle society.

Business models, operations and even the types of businesses that will emerge will be radically different from what we've seen in the past. New skills will be needed, as will different working relationships, support and emotional intelligence.

Maintaining relevance during times of such unprecedented and fundamental change will require you to be clear about who you are, your purpose and values, and the skill sets you bring to any role, your emotional intelligence and your personal brand.

Given many people will have more time on their hands, use this time to think through the concepts in this book and work on brand you.

As Greg Baxter, partner at Newgate Communications, so eloquently commented back in 2018 in an article about the decline in trust:

Being legally right and morally wrong equals being wrong.[1]

So, let's get started.

1 https://www.afr.com/opinion/corporate-reputation-its-character-that-counts-when-the-chips-are-down-20180312-h0xc3w

Part I

YOUR PERSONAL BRAND

1 Establishing and maintaining your relevance

Your brand is what people say about you when you're not in the room.

Your relevance is that you are the person people associate with a specific area of knowledge, insight and influence, and they trust you over time.

The effectiveness of 'brand you' is fundamentally about your *relevance*, as it's through your relevance that you can make an impact. Your relevance is about *what you can do*, not *who you are* – about being *something* not just *someone*.

What exactly do I mean when I use the term 'relevance'? The *Oxford English Dictionary* defines 'relevance' as 'the state of being closely connected or appropriate to the matter in hand'. At its most basic then relevance is simply having meaning or purpose, personally, professionally, or spiritually at a point in time.

To be relevant is thus to be important, but the term implies more than that.

To be *relevant*, an action or person must be connected to a larger scheme, a grander plan – the ultimate 'matter in hand'. As leaders, we should bring meaningful and purposeful solutions to the many perplexing issues in our world.

In the business world, to be relevant means being an integral part of your organisation, of your company, of the economy, and of the future. It means being the kind of person on whom others depend, whether for leadership, expertise, acumen or emotional support.

As with consumer brands, the more relevant you are the more effective you can be and the more impact you can have. To be relevant to someone or to an organisation, you need to understand what is of utmost importance to them, just as a consumer brand or service brand must deeply understand what the customer wants.

The more relevance you have, the more opportunity you have to influence and make an impact for the better, because people who seek you out are more open and willing to listen to your ideas and thoughts and then implement them. This is not to say you are the 'be all and end all' in any given organisation, only that the more relevance you have the more you are able to make a difference. For example, I'm passionate about helping not-for-profit organisations find more sustainable ways to keep helping people. Because of my knowledge of branding and business I'm regarded as being highly relevant to such organisations. My reputation is also such that people know of my commitment to helping others, so that also supports my relevance. If I had left my business role, retired and gone fishing for years, my relevance would be considerably diminished, even though I'd still have the same knowledge and skills.

MORE RELEVANCE EQUALS MORE IMPACT

So how does relevance affect 'brand you'? The value of relevance is in the ability to make an impact at scale.

You might want to change something about your community, company, city, the world – and we all know there are plenty of things that need changing. Let's take something that impacts us all: climate change. You might want to do something to help bring change, but without relevance you're probably limited to recycling at your home, working in a community garden, signing petitions, limiting your own power use – all worthwhile efforts but they do not have an impact at scale. Conversely, if you're a scientist and you become actively engaged in scientific, public and inter-governmental discussions and policy making over a period of time, you'll become more relevant and be able to make a larger impact.

Or, you might want to help improve the lives of women and children in developing countries. Without relevance you've got a range of options that will have an impact on a few lives through donating your time, money or both. If you had greater relevance in the charitable sector, for those organisations that could use your help and with potential donors you could magnify your efforts and make a significant impact. Just think, if you were highly relevant you might be able to secure the support of the Bill & Melinda Gates Foundation and change millions of lives.

The value of relevance can also be seen in the workplace. The more relevant you are in your organisation the more you can effect change, and this doesn't mean you have to be in the executive suite. You might be passionate about more diversity in your organisation but be a relatively new recruit or junior manager. Initially you may not have much relevance, but if you become engaged in the diversity programs within the company, undertake research, and engage with others around this topic through seminars, conferences and online groups, you'll increase your knowledge and relevance within your organisation over time. And then over time you could be promoted into more senior roles with oversight over diversity policies and actions.

The more relevant you are in whatever area you want to make an impact, the more impact you can make.

RELEVANCE AND TIME

The interesting thing about relevance is that you can have relevance *at a moment in time* as well as *over time*, if you manage your reputation well.

Let's have a look.

Relevance at a moment in time

With a consumer brand, if a customer wants, say, a car or television, that's top of mind for only a short period of time. If you're a car brand or television brand, at that time you are relevant when the customer has that need or want, then it's gone.

Similarly with people. The skill sets, attitudes and behaviours you have form your reputation. These are often only relevant to people when they are focused on a specific outcome or goal they want to achieve, and the same goes for companies. An organisation might want a financial controller. There's thousands of financial controllers available, but only a few who are highly relevant at that moment in time. Most individual financial controllers are not relevant as they haven't focused long enough on making sure that they are, focusing more on their skills and not their 'brand'.

Relevance at a moment in time is about being visible and top of mind when the moment occurs.

Relevance over time

This is a fascinating part of our journey through creating a brand new brand you, and forms how I've structured the book.

Each of us have different parts to our lives – some more, some less – that we are relevant in and therefore have more or less impact on, should we choose. For the purposes of exploring relevance over time I've chosen four key areas:

- family
- work
- community
- country.

At any given point in time, your relevance to each of these areas is different and the pathways you travel are different.

Below is a graph that takes you through one relevance journey over time.

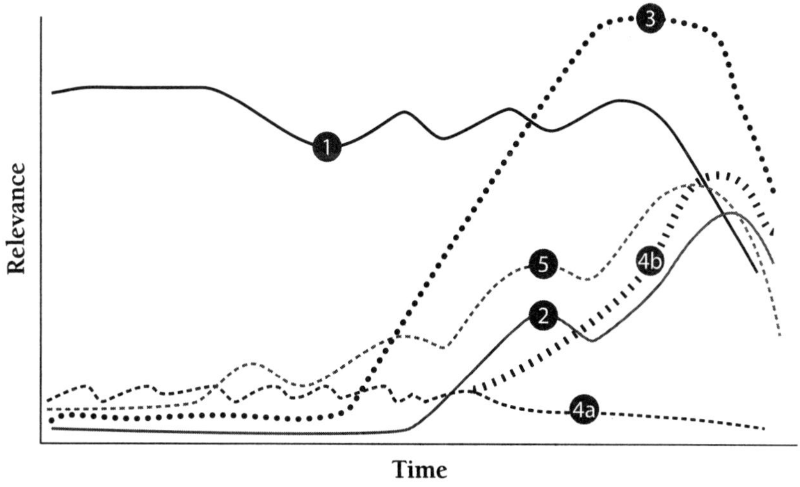

Different pathways depending on:	1. Family 1	4a. Community (not active)
	2. Family 2 (your own)	4b. Community (active)
	3. Business	5. Country (possible)

Let's consider each of these four areas of relevance.

Family

We start out (and mostly maintain) high relevance to our family. When we're born and right through childhood and our late teens we're highly relevant to our parents. As we grow older and become more independent we're less relevant to them (loved, but less relevant) and them to us. As we start our own families (line 2 in the graph above), we become highly relevant to our new family and less relevant to our extended family.

Work

Here we are talking about you as a business participant, not as a consumer. We all start out not being relevant at all in this area. We don't become relevant until we enter the workforce, and if we manage 'brand you' in a proactive way we can become highly relevant for a period of time (a business leader, if you will), and then become less relevant when we leave a company, or perhaps we maintain relevance by becoming an interim executive or board member.

Community

Again we're not relevant at all as a leader in this area until potentially somewhere in our late teens or early 20s, and even then it's only those who actively take part in groups and organisations where leadership skills can be developed before your mid to late 20s (such as sporting teams, Scouts, Guides, cadets, community groups and political parties).

We become more and more relevant as we get older in these groups as our skills and networks grow and our reputation builds. More and more people 'know' about you and seek you out. And, for some, our relevance continues through to later life, post business or work, as we retain engagement with and relevance for the specific groups we have chosen to focus on.

Country

By this I mean representing your country in some way, shape or form, but not sports which would have quite a different pathway.

Most of us are not at all relevant as a leader for our country until well into our 30s, and probably later. Most elected politicians aren't relevant till they are in the higher levels of their party's leadership team or a minister. Most non-elected leaders (administrators, top-level bureaucrats, and trade, defence, security and financial representatives) are well into their 50s and 60s before they are relevant, and even then – given Australia's role in the global political and economic environment – some may question the level of relevance … but that's another discussion.

Relevance for your country (and the world) more often than not increases with age. Think Bill Gates, Warren Buffett, Germaine Greer, Ray Dalio, Andrew Forrest, Elizabeth Evatt, Frank Lowy, David Attenborough, Sir Edmund Hillary, Catherine Livingstone, Graeme Clark … even Harry Vanda and George Young and Angus and Malcolm Young.

It is, however, also fickle, and many lose their relevance overnight when the political scene changes or their term is finished. And there's always exceptions; in terms of age we have Malala Yousafzai and Greta Thunberg. In terms of continuing relevance, Ronald Reagan remains so through the term 'Reaganomics', as does Margaret Thatcher with 'Thatcherism'.

Here you have no relevance for quite some time and then it gradually increases (in most cases), at which time you might have a period of high relevance and then become irrelevant quite quickly, maintain a lower level of relevance, or shift your relevance to focus on business or community.

* * *

Of course, this chart shows just one example of a journey … each person's journey will be slightly – or a lot – different. The point however is that relevance is a journey over time and it changes across the different parts of your life. You can choose to just let it take its own course, or you can be aware of this and actively manage it.

For example, some people think they can maintain relevance with their business relationships when they stop working. But before long they're talking about business issues and dynamics that are from the past and not issues of today and tomorrow. They start talking more and more about what used to be and not about now or the future. They become less and less relevant in business circles.

They become stranded.

Business moves incredibly quickly, even moreso now in the age of digital disruption and global connectivity. As a professional or business person you have to focus on current and emerging trends and knowledge to keep up and maintain relevance. When I stepped out of my CEO role I was very aware of the need to continue to talk about and operate in the here and now and the future, not the past. It takes a conscious effort and requires gaining a deeper understanding of – for example – AI, IoT, cyber security, privacy, cross-border financial and information flows, geopolitics and more.

HOW TO MAINTAIN RELEVANCE OVER TIME

Maintaining relevance over time requires you to:

- make a conscious effort
- be adaptable
- maintain your appearance
- understand and live up to the culture and values you are operating in.

Let's consider each of these issues.

Conscious effort

Maintaining relevance over time takes a conscious effort. More importantly, it requires a level of self-reflection and emotional intelligence, and this leads to a deeper exploration of the real purpose in life. As Simon Sinek has captured in his now iconic TED Talk (and book) about leadership *Start with Why* – which had 48.1 million views the last time I looked – the key to relevance over time is to understand your own personal why and let that drive your decisions.[2] You need to be aware of and understand your own abilities, strengths and weaknesses so you can identify what you need to work on and get guidance about and support with. If you are really in tune with your purpose and know what areas you need to develop this will help to underpin ongoing relevance.

Let's have a look at an example. I'd suggest Roger Federer is a master of relevance *over time*. Over many years he has built up a highly recognised personal brand. He's also mastered relevance *at a point in time* (grand slam finals and wins time and time again). While his relevance may be changing over time due to his age,

2 https://www.ted.com/talks/simon_sinek_how_great_leaders_inspire_action

his performances at a point in time have extended his relevance. Connected to his performance are his strong values. These underpin his reputation, and he's linked with sponsors who share those values.

IBM is perhaps one of the best business examples of actively maintaining relevance over time. In 1984, IBM was the king of the computing world. IBM was successful because it bought hardware components from smaller manufacturers and shipped its PCs pre-loaded with Microsoft Windows. This strategy came unstuck when 'PC clones' flooded the market, built with cheaper components and running the same versions of Windows. In 1993, IBM posted what at the time was the largest loss in the history of corporate America: US$8 billion.

The company had to make a choice: innovate or die. The decision was made to abandon the core of its business model: building and selling low-margin PCs, computer chips, printers and other hardware. IBM's new focus would be providing IT expertise and computing services to businesses.

By 2010, IBM had acquired more than 200 companies in the IT services sector and invested heavily in its server business, becoming the number one seller of enterprise server solutions in the world by 2013. IBM's current investments in artificial intelligence have created a huge stir, placing the company back among the top inventors. Still, the company has plans to further reinvent itself.

Being adaptable

Maintaining relevance also requires being adaptable. Here are a number of people who have maintained relevance over time by being adaptable:

- David Gonski (lawyer, investment banker, board director, ASX Chairman, mentor)

- Janine Ellis (Founder Boost Juice, part owner Retail Zoo)
- General Sir Peter Cosgrove (retired senior Army officer, leader of the taskforce to manage the aftermath of Cyclone Larry to Governor General)
- Imelda Roach (Nutrimetics franchise owner, property developer, Chancellor, Bond University)
- Michelle Simmons (international reputation in quantum computing; Director of the Australian Research Council Centre of Excellence for Quantum Computation & Communication Technology; Australian of the Year 2018)
- Len Bleasel (CEO, ASX Chairman, Foundation Chairman)
- Jim Courier (tennis champion, commentator for the Australian Open, tennis analyst)
- Henry Kissinger (Harvard academic, US Secretary of State, businessman, government adviser)
- Janet Holmes à Court (Chairperson of one of Australia's largest private companies, Heytesbury Pty Ltd, Board member of the Reserve Bank, Pro-Chancellor of the University of Western Australia, Senate member of both Murdoch University and the University of Western Australia).

Those who have *not* maintained relevance over time – some by choice and others due to business failures – include:

- Australian businesspeople Paul Simons, Frank Conroy, Poppy King, John Spalvins, Basil Sellers, Colin Reynolds, Jodee Rich and Rodney Adler
- Australian journalist Jana Wendt

- Australian sports stars Walter Lindrum, Edwin Flack, Dunc Grey and Keith Miller
- Australian brands (not by choice) Rosella, Life Savers, Pongrass boats, Grace Brothers, Darrell Lea, Angus & Robertson, Fosseys, Gowings, and Anthony Hordern, among many others.

Of course, some of you won't recognise these names – and that's exactly my point.

And, of course, there are those who have had relevance, lost it, and then recaptured it or been redeemed. Michael Milken, the American financier who pioneered junk bonds and served a long sentence for violating US securities law, comes to mind. Post his prison term he co-founded the Milken Family Foundation and is chairman of the Milken Institute and founder of medical philanthropies funding research into melanoma, other cancers and other life-threatening diseases. A prostate cancer survivor, Milken has devoted significant resources to research into the disease.[3]

Tiger Woods is an interesting case of shifting relevance and redemption. At one time Tiger was the best golfer in the world, until his fall from grace due to personal issues and then continuing poor performances. Through hard work and the way he dealt with his personal and health issues, he has been somewhat resurrected. He received the Presidential Medal of Freedom, the US's highest civilian honour, in 2019.

Appearance matters

Whether we like it or not, people do judge others by how they present themselves and what's regarded as acceptable in certain

---

3 https://en.wikipedia.org/wiki/Michael_Milken

environments. Consciously and subconsciously, people do assess your relevance to them or to an organisation by how you present yourself. While this has changed to a degree in some parts of the business world – particularly in the tech space, where jeans, chinos and a t-shirt are quite standard – there are still many other places where you'd be regarded as less relevant if you dressed like that.

This is also partly generational and reflective of your age and stage of life. For people of my generation and beyond (over 55) there would be a negative perception if we dressed too casually, but for people in their 40s, 'smart casual' is generally acceptable, as long as you still present yourself professionally. However, I think even in that generation there'd be some surprise if you turned up in board shorts and a t-shirt to a boardroom presentation seeking investment funding, even if you worked for Billabong, Stüssy or a scale-up. In this context there is an expectation that when you're in a boardroom discussing mergers, acquisitions or seeking funding, some appreciation of the gravitas of the situation is required. A level of informality is one thing, but not giving a stuff and being overly casual is another thing altogether.

Culture and values

Adaptability also applies to how you speak and present, and it's linked to understanding the culture you are operating in. It's important not to underestimate cultural mores in relation to relevance. For example, you could be the most competent, skilled person in your field but if you're loud and swear all the time that's going to put some people off at best, offend some, and perhaps even be against company policy. While this may be your personality, it'd be extremely off-putting in most – if not all – business settings.

Culture and relevance are intertwined. You can be perceived to be relevant but be of the wrong culture. If people aren't comfortable with the way you appear, talk or behave, you go right out the door and you cease to be relevant. In addition, your brand becomes that you're known as a foul-mouthed individual with a high degree of intelligence – not someone who you would want to invite home to dinner or out with prospective clients.

Take Australian tennis player Nick Kyrgios. He has a level of recognition, but his behaviour turns people off so his relevance is significantly compromised … as is his ability to earn as much as possible from tennis.

In the 1990s and 2000s, businessman John Elliott's relevance and impact was significantly compromised by his eccentric, crass and abrasive personal style. Jack Welch, the highly regarded head of General Electric, had his reputation severely damaged in the early 2000s when his affair with a *Harvard Business Review* editor came to light, along with an overly generous payout from GE.[4] And then there's Conrad Black, who at one time controlled the world's third-largest English-language newspaper empire (including a minority stake in the *Sydney Morning Herald*, the Melbourne *Age*, and the *Australian Financial Review*). Black was convicted on four counts of fraud in the US in 2007 and served several years in federal prison there. Interestingly, Black was pardoned by President Trump in May 2019.

In recent years, Mark Zuckerberg, co-founder, Chairman and CEO of Facebook, has come under significant pressure due to the lax culture he has created and presided over within Facebook in specific reference to the use and abuse of Facebook data. The Cambridge

---

4 https://www.independent.co.uk/news/world/americas/jack-the-lad-pays-180m-to-keep-his-divorce-and-a-whole-heap-of-dirty-linen-out-of-court-94957.html

Analytica scandal in 2018 severely impacted on his and the company's reputation, as did a massive data breach of Instagram's passwords in 2019. (Facebook owns Instagram.) Statements about how the company is committed to protecting its users' data and monitoring its sites for terrorist and racist content are simply not believed.

More recently, we've seen the rise and demise of Adam Neumann, the co-founder of WeWork. The company was going to list on the sharemarket for US$46 billion at the start of 2019, only to pull the float after the 'mismatch' between what Adam said and did, and issues with its governance and business model. In addition, the related-party transactions involving Neumann and various members of his family, combined with the voting share structure, just didn't add up.[5] By September 2019, Adam had stepped down as CEO and relinquished his preferential voting shares. It remains to be seen if Adam can recover, or if WeWork can ever turn a profit or have a successful IPO. Both Adam's brand and that of WeWork have suffered considerably.

Then there's Harvey Weinstein, the American former film producer who was dismissed from his company – The Weinstein Company – and expelled from the Academy of Motion Picture Arts and Sciences as a result of sexual abuse allegations. In February 2020 he was convicted of a criminal sexual act in the first degree and rape in the third degree. As one of the most powerful men in Hollywood, he had a reputation for ruthlessness and anger. The #MeToo campaign encouraged individuals to share their suppressed stories of sexual misconduct, and unleashed myriad allegations across multiple industries that brought about the swift ouster of many men in positions of power around the world, demolishing their reputations and their careers.

5 https://www.linkedin.com/pulse/corporate-spin-its-best-wework-jaqui-lane/

In sport you don't have to get too far into the Australian NRL season (and sometimes even before the start of the season) to hear about player after player being charged with domestic violence, assault, drug taking, drink driving, and other unacceptable and often illegal behaviour. In fact, court documents from a 2019 case identify that between 2015 and 2018, NRL players were involved in off-field scandals on average every 22 days.[6] Of course, AFL and Rugby Union have also had their fair share of disreputable player and club behaviour. Many sporting careers have ended as a result of the disconnect with what is regarded as acceptable behaviour in society, including those of Todd Carney, Brendan Fevola, Ben Cousins and even whole teams – for example, the Cronulla Sharks ASADA scandal.

Companies have also long been exposed for their lack of values. Back in 1984 it was Union Carbide and the Bhopal gas disaster, the world's worst industrial accident, when over 500,000 people were exposed to a highly toxic gas. In 1989 there was the Exxon Valdez (Exxon Mobil) oil spill, followed by the 2010 Deepwater Horizon disaster (BP) in the Gulf of Mexico. More recently we've seen the impact of mismatched values in the Volkswagen emissions scandal.

All these and other scandals impact on individuals and the company, ruining or severely impacting reputations and therefore reducing their relevance and impact and ability to earn money and to operate effectively.

How you behave and how the company or organisation you work for behaves has a direct impact on you, so maintain your personal standards and choose to work only with people and organisations that share your values and live their culture.

---

6 https://www.msn.com/en-au/sport/rugby-league/court-documents-reveal-an-nrl-scandal-every-22-days-on-average-as-major-sponsors-grow-wary/ar-AAF6VsY

THE IMPORTANCE OF VALUES AND BEHAVIOUR

Executives and CEOs are more and more being judged on their values, or on any divergences between their stated values and their actual behaviour. A worldwide survey of CEO success undertaken by Strategy& and released in 2019 noted: '39% of CEO oustings in 2018 were due to ethical lapses, 35% were due to financial performance and 13% were the result of conflicts with the company's board.' The report states that this breakdown is very different to previous findings: 'At the height of the global financial crisis in 2008, 52% of CEO dismissals were due to financial performance, 35% were due to board conflicts and 10% were due to misconduct.' The growing presence and power of activist investors could be a contributing factor to the higher rate of CEO turnover, the report adds: 'The rise in these kinds of dismissals reflects several societal and governance trends, including more aggressive intervention by regulatory and law enforcement authorities, new pressures for accountability about sexual harassment and sexual assault brought about by the rise of the #MeToo movement, and the increasing propensity of boards of directors to adopt a zero-tolerance stance toward executive misconduct.'[7]

WHAT YOU 'DO' DOES NOT SUSTAIN RELEVANCE

Many people – especially in business, politics and sport – align their view of relevance to what they *do* rather than *who they are*. This can and does create significant challenges when their main role is no longer available, by choice or forced upon them. It's at this point that many people flounder.

---

7 https://aicd.companydirectors.com.au/membership/membership-update/top-5-ceo-turnover-trends-for-boards

We're also living in a fast-paced world where the rate of technological change is rapid. Because each generation of technology improves over the last, the rate of progress from version to version speeds up. As Alison Berman and Jason Dorrier note in their article 'Technology Feels Like It's Accelerating Because It Is':

> *This acceleration can be measured in the 'returns' of the technology – such as speed, efficiency, price-performance, and overall 'power' – which improve exponentially too.*
>
> *Further, as a technology becomes more effective, it attracts more attention. The result is a flood of new resources – such as increased R&D budgets, recruiting top talent, etc. – which are directed to further improving the technology.*
>
> *This wave of new resources triggers a 'second level' of exponential growth, where the rate of exponential growth (the exponent) also begins accelerating.*
>
> *Because the future is approaching much faster than we realize, it's critical to think exponentially about where we're headed and how we'll get there.*[8]

It's also a demanding job and business environment. There are no jobs for life anymore. The average tenure for a CEO in Australia is 4.2 years and the average job tenure is just 3.4 years.[9] There are (and have been for a while) age limits on partners of the leading accounting and advisory firms, usually around the mid-50s. If you're going to live till you're 80 you better be clear about your purpose and where you want to be relevant.

---

8 https://singularityhub.com/2016/03/22/technology-feels-like-its-accelerating-because-it-actually-is/

9 https://www.power2motivate.com.au/news-blog/blog/australian-employment-tenure-is-shrinking

For graduates and younger managers and executives, you need to understand the dynamics of how to become and stay relevant much earlier on in your career so that you can build your relevance earlier and have a greater impact, wherever you work and whatever your skill set. The other critical element to understand is that you need to keep learning and up-skilling. If you're not regularly learning new skills and extending your knowledge you'll become less relevant in your organisation.

In reality everything you touch and every part of your life is a reflection of you, who you are, your purpose and how you express yourself. As you move through the various aspects of your life and relevance journeys, what will sustain you and help you maintain relevance in those areas that you wish to develop is your purpose.

2 Defining your values

'We can afford to lose money – even a lot of money. But we can't afford to lose reputation – even a shred of reputation.' – Warren Buffett memo to employees at Berkshire Hathaway 2014

In the business world there is a whole industry built around branding and brand value, the brands themselves, advertisers, marketing professionals and companies that measure brand value. Two of the most recognisable reports on brands are the 'Interbrand Best Global Brands' report and the 'Edelman Trust Barometer'. They are eagerly awaited each year, and form much of how companies assess how their brands are going.

However, when it comes to your personal brand, when I ask about your brand value I don't mean in monetary terms, I'm talking about your values. Your values make up your value. Your brand takes a lifetime to build – and just seconds to lose. Just look at Dominique Strauss-Kahn, Rolf Harris, Bill Cosby, Sepp Blatter and George Pell.

VALUES AND ETHICS

Values are different from but linked to ethics. It's important to understand the difference in terms of understanding your personal values. Everybody has a certain set of values and a certain code of ethics that are very much valued. They are the basic beliefs that an individual thinks to be true. Every individual has a set of values through which he or she looks at all things and also at the world. It can be said that most people will never deviate from their values. Values can be said to be the guiding principles in one's life. Ethics are guidelines or rules that are set for a society or an organisation rather than for an individual. Ethics are mainly based on moral values which are based on virtues, rights and obligations.[1]

The values you bring to 'brand you' and your brand value will help to define the success you achieve across all aspects of your life that relate to family, friends, community and work. Gone are the days when you could 'fake it till you make it'. Social media and the speed at which news travels have opened up everyone to accountability in a way that simply didn't exist even 15 years ago.

Values are often described as 'core' and 'secondary'. Core values are strong and not changeable, whereas secondary values are open to change if you experience, engage or research a different perspective that changes your view. Your core values are what drive everything you do, why you do it, how you do it and who you choose to engage with at all stages of your life.

The dynamics of your personal brand are instilled from an early age, initially unconsciously through your parents and close family. As you grow you start to form your own sense of values, and sometimes this can bring you into conflict with family, friends and others.

---

1 http://www.differencebetween.net/language/difference-between-ethics-and-values/

These can be challenging times. By the time you're in your mid-20s your values have been largely formed, although you're likely to be tested on these over the next 10 to 20 years of business, work and life. How you deal with these challenges will crystallise your values, as you may have to make a stand based on these values. By your late 40s and into your 50s, your values are well set, but are not immoveable if you are open to new information, insights and experiences. Sometimes one of the hardest things we have to do personally is confront a long-held value and decide that it's not something we wish to continue with.

Given this book is focused on those working in and around business and community organisations, it's important to recognise that your value is not about who you know but about who 'you' are. Networks, of course, are important in business and life but they can only get you so far. They might open doors, but once you've walked through them it's you and your brand value that will determine what kind of reception you get and the level of influence you bring to bear to these new relationships.

Some consumer behaviour research proposes there are six internal values and three external values. They are self-respect, warm relationships, sense of accomplishment, self-fulfilment, fun and enjoyment, excitement, sense of belonging, being well respected, and security.[2] I think these, while workable for consumer research, are not specific or strong enough descriptors for personal values. So, let's look into this a little further.

---

2 Wayne D. Hoyer; Deborah J. MacInnis; Rik Pieters (2012). *Consumer Behavior*. Cengage Learning. p. 395.

SO, WHAT ARE YOUR VALUES?

Over decades I've ask this question to hundreds of businesspeople and community leaders. Most are unable to answer it clearly. Values are something we often take as given, and we live by them without ever consciously exploring or articulating them. But I believe it's critically important in terms of understanding 'brand you' – your reputation and relevance over time – to clearly identify your values.

Part of the purpose of this book is to encourage you to deeply explore what your values are and why they are important to you. Here are some of mine:

- honesty
- reliability
- transparency
- authenticity
- loyalty
- excellence
- sensitivity
- giving back
- accountability
- fairness.

What are some of yours? Write them down now and then explore why they are your values, whether they have ever been tested, and if so, what action did you take? How did this make you feel? What was the result? You might also group them into core and secondary values: what you will not compromise on, and what you would re-evaluate based on new experiences, information or changing cultural ethics.

Part of this discussion is to work out what's negotiable or tradable and what's not. You will be tested at various points in your life, so it's important to understand what's an immutable value and what's not, what's a core value and what's a secondary one. For example: what would you do if you knew someone in your company was bullying someone in a junior position? Would you offer to assist and support the junior person? Confront the senior person? Report the situation? Do nothing? If one of your values was accountability or even authenticity or sensitivity, you'd take action. What action might be dependent on the particular company's policies and practices in relation to bullying.

Some examples

Let me share an example that many might face in an increasingly contract-based environment.

An executive shared with a contractor that they wanted to get rid of one of the people the contractor was working with as they didn't like them. The contractor felt hugely conflicted. They needed the contract but had worked with and developed a good relationship with the person in question. Should they tell this person? How would they react? What would the potential consequences be if they took action against the executive? After three days, the contractor decided to share the information with the person and accept whatever consequences. The value of honesty and fairness overrode the potential commercial damage.

In my former role as CEO of a company we were offered the licence for a popular brand that would have added significantly to our revenue and profitability. However, the culture and values of the representative of the company did not sit well with me, particularly the way they wanted to present their product to consumers.

They wanted to market their product as 'pure' when in fact it was not – they wanted to create labelling and marketing that was opaque enough so it inferred it was pure. This did not align with my values, and we declined the offer along with the subsequent $30 million in revenue that came with it. Interestingly, the brand only lasted four years before its demise and millions of dollars spent in Australia.

Another example comes from the not-for-profit space when I came on as Chairman at a new organisation. One of the board members was not aligned with the values and culture of the board and organisation; they wanted to put themselves ahead of the vision of the business. Their whole ethical and moral approach to participating was totally unaligned to their colleagues and peers.

It took me five minutes to work out what the issue was, and much longer to work through a solution. I tried to manage it the best I could by engaging with the individual, trying to bring them into the fold and using techniques I'd learnt to support their self-esteem and ego. My efforts did not work, and the individual continued to destabilise the board. I had to work through a more drastic approach that caused the individual to make a choice as to whether his reputation would be questioned based on his behaviour in the boardroom. The penny dropped, and the solution I gave him allowed him to depart gracefully (in his opinion).

Another instance was a board scenario where as Chairman I believed there were a number of board members not behaving with what I regarded as the right moral and ethical approach in the boardroom. However, I was not able to engage the support of other board members, who were preoccupied with other issues. I had two options: wage 'all-out war' with the individuals who did not recognise or appreciate my point of view, and have this impact the whole boardroom and organisation, or leave. Others on the board saw what was happening, but the problem was too challenging for them to deal with immediately. I decided the best course of action for me personally and the organisation was to make the change that was aligned to my values, so I retired.

The lesson I learned (again) was that the values of those in the leadership team (board and executive) need to be aligned. If they are not, there's only one solution ... change the people.

Living by your values is, in some cases, extremely difficult. You might lose a contract, job or position for following your values. You might lose some friends or even family. Living by your values means you will have to make choices rather than walk away, not speak up, not take responsibility. Consider the whistleblower in a company, community organisation or government. They put at risk their entire career because of their values. But living without your values is impossible. If you compromise on your values, you don't stand for anything.

VALUES IN CONTEXT

Over time, the public expression of personal values that groups of people find important in their day-to-day lives lay the foundations of laws, customs and traditions. They are the norms we all live by. Different cultures and countries have different norms, which makes it challenging when you're working in a global company, organisation or as a businessperson working with virtual teams and individuals.

In addition, the world has changed considerably over recent years. Ten years ago businesspeople and the community largely didn't judge people outside their primary domain, whether that be business, sports or politics (spies and indiscrete politicians excepted). There was an unwritten code that someone's personal life was just that, personal. That's now all gone. Social media and the speed at which the private can become public has resulted in a sea change in what is now considered public … which is pretty much anything. Trial by social media – right or wrong – is a significant part of modern context, therefore active awareness and management of your brand, reputation and relevance means careful consideration of social media across all its platforms.

In terms of 'brand you', your values will be seen in context through the way you behave. It's one thing to have values, it's another to live by them all the time. Let's look at a few more examples from different fields.

Tiger Woods is regarded as one of the greatest golfers ever. He was the top-ranked golfer in the world from August 1999 to September 2004, and again from June 2005 to October 2010 (281 weeks). Woods's 'office was the golf course', but it was his behaviour outside the 'office' that conflicted with the values and behaviour 'at the office'. Even though his behaviour in the public eye was impeccable, he was brought down by what could be considered private indiscretions.

Australian tennis player Nick Kyrgios's behaviour on court displays values that are inconsistent with the values of the tennis profession and wider community. No matter how good a tennis player he is, in the context of community expectations he doesn't cut it.

Some Australian cricketers' actions – specifically Steve Smith, David Warner and Cameron Bancroft – in tampering with the ball during a test match against South Africa in 2017 were a clear example of values in context. All involved paid a very high price for breaching the standards of behaviour expected of them.

There's plenty of examples in the business world as well, so let's take just two.

Harvey Weinstein, CBE (yes, he was made an honorary CBE in 2004) was once one of the world's leading entertainment moguls through his company Miramax Films. His studio produced some of the most successful movies of the past 30 years, such as *Pulp Fiction*, *Heavenly Creatures* and *Shakespeare in Love*, as well as many musicals and plays. Many actors' careers were launched and grew as a result. In October 2017, all this came crashing down as a result of sexual assault allegations, over 80 by the end of that month. The #MeToo movement was sparked from this and has resulted in other high-profile denouements. The 'Weinstein effect' has changed the context in relation to sexual abuse worldwide, and Miramax was forced into bankruptcy and shut down in 2018.

We also have examples closer to home, many of which have been highlighted through the 2018 Royal Commission into Misconduct in the Banking, Superannuation and Financial Services Industry. Many of the banks' and financial institutions' values were *not* about helping customers with their financial or personal security but rather about generating fees, even to the extent of charging dead people. There was little, if any, concern about the impact of these behaviours on the reputation of the banks – the boards and executives were too arrogant.

AMP management and board knew that it was charging dead people insurance premiums; many of the superannuation companies knew they were charging young people with low balances for life insurance they didn't need through the automatic opt-in clause; CBA and other banks were engaged in 'fees for no service' across their wealth management businesses, as well as irresponsible lending practices and more.

The values espoused by the banks and other financial services companies were mostly unaligned with the practices deployed across the companies to capture fees, charges and new business at the expense of customers. This was *after* the Future of Financial Advice (FOFA) reforms in 2013 which were designed to improve the trust and confidence of Australian retail investors in the financial services sector and ensure the availability, accessibility and affordability of high-quality financial advice!

In the world of consumer brands, the value of what a brand stands for is now closely linked to where they source their raw materials, how they treat their workers, and what they are doing in terms of climate change. Twenty years ago some of these issues were of little or no concern to most major companies. Now, companies around the world have to demonstrate what actions they are undertaking across all these areas and more, either by government regulation or consumer demand or both. A brand that hasn't shifted its value proposition to address these issues is out of step with the consumer and will be punished and lose relevance.

For example, fashion label Oroton went into voluntary administration after being in business for 80 years as it failed to keep its brand relevant in the face of increasing competition from other brands and online outlets. It's recently undergone a brand refresh, seeking to reconnect and become relevant to a new generation. It will be interesting to see if it can achieve this in such a competitive retail environment.

Coca-Cola has been facing an ongoing relevance challenge as consumer sentiment moves from sugar-based drinks to healthier options. Coca-Cola moved, albeit perhaps way too late, when it acquired bottled water companies and then created Coke Zero, and latterly moved into sports and energy drinks. However, the company faces another challenge in terms of its value proposition in relation to the pollution caused by single-use plastic. They're forever playing catch up, health-washing and green-washing their brands. Similarly, cigarette companies and more recently oil companies as they contend with their impact on the climate and the increasing consumer push for renewable energy sources.

Politics all over the world is replete with examples of values in context, although it's more challenging to assess as different cultures have different values and we need to be very careful not to overlay a Western values construct over different cultures. Here in Australia, abuse of parliamentary expense claims has cost more than a few politicians their careers, and the superhighway of politicians moving into the Big Four accounting firms and other lucrative boardroom positions and consultancies is of considerable concern to many. And if you think we have a problem in Australia (Julie Bishop and Christopher Pyne being two of the most recent examples), read Richard Brooks's book *Bean Counters: The triumph of the accountants and how they broke capitalism* which, among other things, provides the background to LuxLeaks, and an extensive list of former UK ministers and politicians now working with the very accounting firms they engaged on multi-million-dollar consulting projects.[3]

Another aspect of knowing your values is consistently living by them across all facets of your life: family, business and community. We all know people who regularly say one thing and do another; they are people we regard as unreliable, untrustworthy and lacking in credibility. We are unlikely to recommend them to others as they would reflect badly on us, and we're unlikely to entrust them with business opportunities, advancement in the company or representation on community organisations.

---

3 Brooks, Richard, *Bean Counters: The triumph of the accountants and how they broke capitalism*, Atlantic Books, 2018.

I say 'unlikely to' because in some cases people do continue to support others who are inconsistent with their values and actions. This may be because they are long-time friends, are in a position of power that could assist with our own advancement, they have the capacity to hinder our advancement, or because the inconsistency is something we decide we can live with. Again, knowing your own values clearly is a way of working through such scenarios. There'll be some values you won't compromise on and others you are prepared to re-evaluate. Just be clear exactly what you are considering and why.

From a personal branding perspective however, inconsistency in what you say your values are and what you do is damaging. Let's take some examples across the triumvirate of sport, business and consumer branding.

For years Andre Agassi was one of the bad boys of tennis. Agassi reached the world number one ranking for the first time in 1995, but was troubled by personal issues during the mid to late 1990s and sank to number 141 in 1997. His behaviour was inconsistent with the values of the sport he earned a living from, and certainly impacted on his tennis performance.

Interestingly, he worked long and hard to shift perceptions about him, and in 1999 returned to number one and enjoyed the most successful run of his career over the next four years. In 2001, his foundation (through which he has raised US$117 million) opened the Andre Agassi College Preparatory Academy in Los Vegas, a K–12 public charter school for at-risk children.

Similarly, Tiger Woods has had a turbulent career over the past decade, with his brand damaged seemingly beyond repair at one point. While his golf prowess seems to be returning more recently, it was the inconsistency between his behaviour and his brand values that damaged the Tiger Woods brand.

In business there's the case of Perrier mineral water. A highly successful worldwide brand in 1992, American regulators in North Carolina discovered bottles had been contaminated with benzene, albeit in minuscule quantities that would not affect human health. No one suffered as a result of drinking the benzene-contaminated water, but Perrier recalled 160 million bottles from 120 countries at a cost of over US$250 million. Within 18 months, its market share had declined from 15% to 9% in the US and dropped from 49% to less than 30% in the UK. The share price fell by 37%, and the company was taken over by Nestlé. By 1995, Perrier sales had fallen to 50% of their 1989 peak.[4]

At a completely different scale, in Australia we have the more recent example of Belle Gibson. Apart from the legalities surrounding her false cancer claims and fraudulent activities with her charity, the inconsistencies between her brand promises and values underpinned the sham. While the two were perceived to be aligned, her health app was transformed into a highly successful book and she was in discussions with Apple to transition the app as a pre-installed default third-party inclusion in the Apple Watch's April 2015 launch. Of course, all of this collapsed, and her book published by Penguin was pulped.

Inconsistencies between what you say and your actions also cross over to community and not-for-profit organisations. Many may not remember John Friedrich and the National Safety Council of Australia. Having joined the organisation in 1977, he subsequently became the executive director and built up the company with loans

4 https://www.prweek.com/article/1357209/lessons-learn-product-recall

in which 27 banks agreed to lend millions of dollars. Awarded an OAM in 1988, he was later discovered to be a complete fraudster and was charged with fraud totalling $269 million. It was later discovered that Friedrich was not an Australian citizen, did not possess any valid birth certificate, and did not appear on any electoral roll. Among other things, this caused considerable embarrassment to the Department of Defence, which had given him a security clearance and almost unlimited access to Australian Air Force bases.[5]

More recently the Catholic and other churches, Scouts and various state-run institutions have come under intense public scrutiny because of the lack of consistency in their preaching, teaching and responsibility for those under their care. The Royal Commission into Institutional Responses to Child Sexual Abuse has exposed institutionalised and endemic mistreatment of some of the most vulnerable in our community, and significantly damaged the trust the community has in these organisations.[6]

The inconsistent application of values can also play out in industry and community organisations. The recent machinations at CPA Australia – one of the professional accreditation bodies for accountants in Australia – saw its high-profile (and very well paid and promoted) CEO terminated, along with its Chairman and several board members, after the salary of the CEO, Alex Malley, and other payments to board members came to light. This on top of significant marketing expenditure on Malley's book *The Naked CEO*, and a failed financial advice start-up that competed with many of its members' businesses. Many members and the wider community judged these and other actions to be inconsistent with the values of

---

5 https://en.wikipedia.org/wiki/John_Friedrich_(fraudster)

6 https://www.childabuseroyalcommission.gov.au/sites/default/files/final_report_-_preface_and_executive_summary.pdf

the organisation. As one report noted, the fact that accountants are meant to help improve the financial situations of others made 'the lack of accountability, and financial clarity, from the top accounting body in Australia – CPA Australia – all the more incongruous'.[7]

The subsequent review of the board, the CPA's structure, and board and executive remuneration have gone some way to bringing back alignment between the promoted values of CPA Australia and its actions, however this is an ongoing process and will require a consistent and transparent approach to rebuild the brand of the previously highly regarded organisation both with its members and the business community.

In another example of poor behaviour within an organisation, in June 2014 SES Commissioner Murray Kear resigned after the Independent Commission Against Corruption (ICAC) found he had acted corruptly. Four years later a court found that ICAC 'ran an improper investigation' against Kear, having 'withheld exculpatory evidence and initiated a criminal prosecution against him without reasonable cause'. Magistrate Greg Grogin severely criticised ICAC in two judgments that were never challenged in the courts and which acquitted Mr Kear of the criminal charges initiated by ICAC.[8]

VALUES AND COURAGE

You must have courage to live by your values. Courage has to be part of your language in terms of the decisions you make, the people you associate with (or not), what you will accept (or not), and your

---

7 https://www.smh.com.au/business/alex-malley-cpa-australias-naked-ceo-who-walked-off-with-49m-20170622-gww5jx.html

8 https://www.theaustralian.com.au/business/legal-affairs/icac-is-attempting-to-retry-me-murray-kear/news-story/e7b42a3fad52038f7bd97131300114a9

actions. Consciously thinking about, discussing and articulating your values will provide you with a strong and clear baseline for such decisions and actions, and it's often useful to have these discussions with a mentor or trusted colleague.

Living your values means making a whole range of decisions – some small, some significant – relating to who you work for and with, who you will associate with, and what you will do when faced with challenging situations at work, within your family and friend network, and in other networks you choose to engage with. One of the toughest decisions you may need to make is to take action on behaviour and practices that occur within the company you work for if they don't align with your personal values, if they are against your company's code of conduct or, at the extreme, if they break the law.

We've seen numerous recent examples of employees who have become whistleblowers against poor organisational behaviour. Some suffered significant adverse personal and professional impact:

- In 2016 a joint Four Corners/Fairfax investigation uncovered various practices within CommInsure highlighted by its Chief Medical Officer Dr Koh. Dr Koh was later terminated by CommInsure.[9]
- In 2012 Witness K raised concerns about a covert Australian Secret Intelligence Service operation he ran to bug East Timor's cabinet in 2004 during negotiations about an oil and gas treaty. Bernard Collaery, who once served as ACT Attorney General, and who is representing Witness K, has been prosecuted by

9 https://www.abc.net.au/news/2016-03-07/comminsure-scandal-whos-who-four-corners/7226576

the Federal Government, along with Witness K.[10] The case is ongoing at the time of publication, some eight years after Witness K came forth.

- In 2012 GlaxoSmithKlein made the largest Medicare and Medicaid fraud settlement ever in the US. The whistleblowers – Thomas Gerahty, a former senior marketing development manager for Glaxo, and Matthew Burke, a former regional vice president for Glaxo – provided invaluable insider information alleging that the London-based pharmaceutical company was engaging in corrupt nationwide schemes to push sales of Advair, Wellbutrin, Imitrex and other popular prescription drugs for unapproved uses, that it used improper financial inducements to market its drugs, and that it misrepresented the safety and efficacy of those drugs. Glaxo's illegal practices caused Medicare, Tricare – the healthcare program for the military – and Medicaid to incur huge losses.[11]
- More recently, in 2017 Sally McDow, a highly credentialed lawyer and former senior compliance manager at Origin Energy, lodged the first ever case in Australia that tested whistleblower protections under the Corporations Act, alleging significant and dangerous compliance breaches, a deliberate cover-up by management and potential breaches of the Corporations Act.

Whistleblowing is a tough decision, even with the new Enhancing Whistleblower Protections laws that came into effect on 1 July 2019

---

10 https://www.abc.net.au/news/2018-06-28/witness-k-and-bernard-collaery-charged-intelligence-act-breach/9919268

11 https://www.phillipsandcohen.com/whistleblowers-played-major-role-in-glaxo-case-leading-to-glaxo-s-record-settlement/

through amendments to the Corporations Act.[12] ASIC has its own set of whistleblower protections that are worth reviewing.[13]

The reality is most of us will face much less public or potentially damaging decisions in relation to how we draw on our values to live our life and in the way we conduct ourselves in business and the community. In most instances the decisions you make will form part of a conversation with yourself, in others you might seek advice and guidance from a mentor.

Don't do anything you wouldn't like to read or your family to read on the front page of the newspaper.

VALUES AND VIGILANCE

It's one thing to be clear on your values and how you act, it's another thing altogether to have a wider radar to scan and assess the values of those around you. The reality is that damage to your brand can come from places and people or events you least expect. 'Brand you' can be damaged by association.

As with consumer brands, the values of people and brands can change overnight or over time, so you need to be aware of this and not 'set and forget' your values radar. For example, a person or company may be perceived by you as aligned to your values at a point in time, but change over time or as a result of a specific event or series of events over which you have no knowledge or control, and this could damage your brand. Would you have stuck with Bernie Madoff? Would you have stayed with the now defunct consulting firm Arthur Andersen after it was convicted of obstruction of justice for shredding documents relating to the Enron scandal? (Even though

12 https://www.legislation.gov.au/Details/C2019A00010

13 https://asic.gov.au/about-asic/asic-investigations-and-enforcement/whistleblowing/

the decision was later overturned on a technicality, there was clearly something amiss inside Arthur Andersen.) How about hanging in there with Union Carbide after the Bhopal disaster, Volkswagen post the emissions tampering violations, Storm Financial, AMP, NAB and others?

Closer to home, literally and figuratively, look at the damage done to a former Deputy Commissioner of the ATO, Michael Cranston, who was found not guilty of using his position to benefit his son, Adam Cranston (the Plutus payroll scam – ongoing at the time of publication).

Another example is Dick Smith, the person and brand. Dick Smith sold his company to Woolworths back in 2006. It was subsequently acquired by Anchorage Capital and re-floated, but was placed into administration in 2013. At this point Dick Smith had not been associated with the company that bore his name for more than eight years. A dynamic and high-profile businessperson, many consumers still associated the man with his business and its collapse.

And just think about those who work in the big four banks, Macquarie, IOOF, AMP and others, the majority of whom are no doubt decent, hardworking people. Association with these brands, for some, is not something they see as aligned with their values, for others it is.

The challenge I'm posing here is that you need to – we all need to – make decisions about who we associate with. Our associations are so important for our own personal brand. The choices you make about who to associate with might be right today and a liability tomorrow. The choices you make are critical.

With all decisions there are consequences. Make the right decisions based on your values for the long term. I fully appreciate that this may well have consequences in terms of financial outcome. I've made many such decisions, such as the example I gave earlier when I was CEO of a business and turned down the opportunity of representing a well-known international brand in Australia that would have delivered $30 million in revenue and considerable profits over the period of the licence.

When faced with decisions about your values – your brand – doing nothing is not an option. You need to make a decision and act on it. Not making a choice is a failure to live by your values which will be demonstrated through an inconsistency in your actions and behaviour.

3 The importance of your behaviour

Personal branding is your relevance linked with your reputation. As I've said before, if your reputation is damaged through your behaviour, you could lose credibility, status, influence, income, colleagues, friends and even family. There are countless examples across the worlds of business, entertainment, sports, arts, politics and the community. And, sometimes, the damage to your reputation can occur even when allegations are later proved unsubstantiated. Take the recent cases of Geoffrey Rush (allegations of sexual harassment), Elmer Funke Kupper (who was in executive limbo for over three-and-a-half years after allegations of bribery within Tabcorp; the AFP closed its investigation in September 2019[1]) and John McGuigan (former global Chairman of Baker McKenzie and director of Cascade Coal).[2]

---

1 https://www.theaustralian.com.au/business/companies/elmer-funke-kupper-relieved-at-end-of-tabcorp-bribery-probe/news-story/96aed62558c3eacfbfa065f61930c080

2 https://www.theaustralian.com.au/business/legal-affairs/icacs-narrative-is-demolished/news-story/36a5f6ab8f4fe024cd3b4da83c240fc6

CHANGING EXPECTATIONS OVER TIME

Your reputation and 'brand you' develop and change over time in conscious and unconscious ways. A key part of 'brand you' is exhibited through your behaviours, which are informed by your values. If your behaviours are inconsistent with your values this sends out mixed signals and will damage your brand, so your behaviours are vitally important.

As you mature it's up to you to modify or change your behaviours. You don't have the option to keep the same behaviours as you'll become irrelevant. For example, the way you behave at 25 will be different from 45 or 65.

At age 15 friends, family and colleagues are willing to accept some inconsistencies in your behaviours and varying degrees of social experimentation.

At 25 there's an expectation that you will have grown out of some, if not all, of your more risky social behaviours and adopted a more considered and serious approach to work, reliability, application, energy and diligence. Turning up late for work on a consistent basis is not regarded as acceptable behaviour, neither is incomplete or non-delivery of work requirements. You might be given some leeway, but not much.

There are certainly clear requirements around your interactions with colleagues, customers and clients, in terms of complying with company policies relating to respecting other people, inclusion and mutual safety. Intimidating and bullying behaviour is not acceptable in any workplace, neither is racism or sexual discrimination. If you have beliefs or values that run counter to these and other workplace requirements you'll need to reassess your values and change your behaviours.

By 45, there are clear expectations around how you behave with those who report to you and those you are reporting to. There's also greater expectation around your behaviour in relation to accepting responsibility for outcomes, accountability, taking on more responsibility and representing the organisation.

Again, if you want to be regarded as a leader in your organisation and outside it in community organisations, there is an expectation you will 'step up' and take on more responsibility. If you don't, you risk becoming less relevant across these areas.

Then, as you reach your late 40s through to your 60s there are clear – and high – expectations about your communication and leadership skills, ability to be decisive, and ability to bring together groups of colleagues or parts of your network to achieve larger goals.

In addition, there's now an expectation from workplaces around out-of-work behaviour, especially if it's shared through social media. Plenty of people have been terminated from their employment as a result of behaviours outside the workplace that are inconsistent with their company's values.

CHANGING SOCIETAL NORMS

The norms of society are also constantly changing, as are our laws, so it's important that you actively work on reassessing some of your behaviours if they are out of step with society, even if this means re-evaluating some of your own values. For example, child labour was acceptable and common practice in the 1800s in England and is still practised in some countries around the world today. In most Western countries and many Asian countries child labour is illegal. If your personal view is that child labour is acceptable, you would need to either contain or modify your view when working with a wide range of companies. It may also be a requirement of working in some roles that you actively take steps to ensure no child labour is used in your supply chain.

Or, you may hold views about the role of women in the workforce, or in certain occupations. If so, you would be in breach of various laws of Australia and policies of most companies if you discriminated against women.

Personal behaviour

In Australia at the time of writing there is significant discussion around freedom of speech and the right to express personal religious beliefs. Israel Folau's case against Rugby Australia is the subject of significant debate across business and the wider community, as is the Federal Government's Religious Discrimination Bill.[3] Whatever your personal viewpoint, you need to reassess it in light of the current and pending anti-discrimination laws of this country.

Similarly, what is regarded as acceptable behaviour changes over time. Just look at Harvey Weinstein, who used to tell people, 'I know what I can do'. He clearly knew what he thought he could get away with, until he couldn't. #MeToo changed that, and shifted the entertainment industry's tacit acceptance of a whole raft of exploitative and sexual harassment behaviours.

Company behaviour

The same applies to companies.

In 1996 *Life* magazine published a photo of a young child stitching footballs that carried the Nike logo. The company's reputation suffered, and the first of many protests took place. Nike was one

3 https://www.afr.com/politics/federal/business-fears-israel-folau-religious-freedom-law-20190911-p52q9d

of thousands of companies that had outsourced the manufacture of its products to companies in developing countries and took no responsibility for who their products were actually made by. In 1998 the founder of Nike, Phil Knight, admitted 'the Nike product has become synonymous with slave wages, forced overtime and arbitrary abuse'. Nike and child labour had become indelibly linked in the public consciousness.

As a result, the company started to introduce audits and monitor its supply chain, but in 2006 a similar photo was made public, this time of Pakistani children stitching Nike balls. This time Nike decided to recall the balls and cancel the supplier's contract, at a cost of US$100 million.[4] In 2020 it's now one of the most admired companies in the world in its sector, as are Starbucks and Patagonia, both of which have had their own problems with sourcing coffee and clothing from companies using forced labour, modern slavery and substandard working conditions and treatment.[5]

Another example is that of conflict diamonds, which are diamonds that are mined through violent and illegal means. These diamonds are then sold to fund civil wars and terrorism. This illegal trade has fuelled brutality and war in places such as Sierra Leone, Angola and the Democratic Republic of Congo, where rebels and warmongers controlled civilians and breached human rights.

In 2003, the United Nations established an initiative to prevent diamond sales from funding violence. The Kimberley Process Certification Scheme imposes requirements on participants to certify that shipments of rough diamonds are conflict-free. The purpose of

---

4 http://mallenbaker.net/article/clear-reflection/nike-and-child-labour-how-it-went-from-laggard-to-leader

5 https://www.inc.com/anna-hensel/patagonia-pledges-to-implement-higher-standards-in-factories.html

the scheme is to prevent conflict diamonds from entering the market and being sold, which would in turn evaporate criminal funding. This initiative also protects individuals from unknowingly purchasing conflict diamonds.

Today, conflict diamonds are estimated to account for less than 1% of world diamond production.

And there's the significant issue of child labour. The International Labor Organisation estimates there are over 170 million children engaged in child labour, and while this has declined 30% between 2000 and 2012, it is still rife throughout some of the poorest countries in the world.[6] Consumers have led a backlash against companies that do not monitor their supply chains effectively, including fair trade in coffee production and in cocoa sourcing, as well as companies that use palm oil in their products given the resulting destruction of habitats for orangutans and other flora and fauna.

However, there are still a number of well-known brands that remain under the spotlight for not taking thorough enough action in terms of their supply chain management, including Nestlé, Apple, H&M, Microsoft, New Look and Philip Morris.

Investigations into H&M show they have been using child labour in Myanmar, Bangladesh and Cambodia – and paying as little as 13 pence an hour, although it has substantially improved its supply chain practices since this time. Similarly, in 2013 following the discovery that a Chinese contractor was employing 74 minors, Apple also admitted that its bestselling iPhone X product was being made by schoolchildren.

---

6 https://labs.theguardian.com/unicef-child-labour/

Here in Australia, retailers Coles and Woolworths have dramatically improved their ethical supply chain policies and oversight as well as responsible and sustainable sourcing policies in recognition of demand from their customers.

In 2019 the sixth 'Ethical Fashion Report' graded 130 Australian companies from A to F, based on the efforts undertaken by each company to mitigate the risks of forced labour, child labour and worker exploitation in their supply chains, as well as to protect the environment from the harmful impacts of the fashion industry.[7] Companies that topped the list included Etiko, Freeset, Icebreaker, Kowtow and Outland Denim, while companies that scored an F rating included Camilla & Marc, Lowes, Trelise Cooper, Pingpong, and Jasmine and Will.

Then there's the rise of 'B Corp' companies. Certified B companies balance purpose and profit and are legally required to consider the impact of their decisions on workers, customers, suppliers, community and the environment.[8] Australian B Corps include:

- Aspen Medical
- Three Sista's
- McGeoch Birkdale Nursery
- EcoSTEPS
- Catalyser
- Flow Hive
- Pablo & Rusty's

---

7 https://www.business-humanrights.org/en/australia-ethical-fashion-report-grades-130-companies-based-on-efforts-to-mitigate-forced-labour-child-labour-exploitation-in-supply-chains

8 https://bcorporation.com.au/

- Biome Eco Stores
- Pozible
- Stone & Wood Brewing
- Who Gives a Crap
- Dumbo Feather.

THE DYNAMICS OF REPUTATION

> *'All you have in life is your reputation: you may be very rich, but if you lose your good name, then you'll never be happy. The thought will always lurk at the back of your mind that people don't trust you.'* – Richard Branson

Reputations are made up of formal and informal ingredients. Let's have a look at each.

Formal ingredients

Formal elements include official qualifications, institution imprimaturs and endorsements from powerful people.

Official qualifications

'Official qualifications' is really another description for honing your skills. Malcolm Gladwell in his book *Outliers: The story of success* refers to this as the 10,000 hours argument. You need time to learn and develop your skills out of the spotlight before you apply them in your workplace or in other organisations, whether they are sporting, community, political … whatever. For example, the Beatles tested themselves in Hamburg by playing to different audiences for up to eight hours a night before they ventured further afield.

Institutional recognition

Institutional recognition is also important, although it does vary across industry sectors and some people have become highly regarded leaders without any formal qualifications, but they're the exception. Tertiary education is an important start in many fields, as is membership of the relevant industry associations and bodies. (In some sectors registration with these associations is a requirement of being able to work in that area.) And some institutions have a higher level of recognition than others or value level than others. For example, a business or management degree from Harvard, MIT, Oxford, Cambridge, London School of Economics or INSEAD is regarded more highly than one from a lesser known university such as University of Wisconsin, UCLA, University of Texas or an online university.

Other institutions or organisations that may be relevant in the Australian context are:

- the Australian Institute of Company Directors
- CPA Australia (although it's been through a challenging time recently and is perhaps not as highly regarded as it once was)
- the CEO Institute
- TEC (The Executive Connection)
- CEDA (Committee for Economic Development of Australia)
- the Lowy Institute
- Rotary
- YPO (Young Presidents Organization)
- the Business Council of Australia
- the Private Wealth Network.

Others include business clubs and golf clubs, where in some cases membership is highly sought after. For some, political party membership is regarded as an important group.

Endorsements from powerful people

Endorsement from highly regarded leaders in your field or area of community interest is also an important element of formal recognition. There's a saying that elephants marry elephants. If a highly regarded business or community leader supports and endorses you they are attaching their reputation to yours, effectively saying, 'I believe this person is someone that I would associate or work with, and I think others should as well'.

This can also apply to the company you work with. For example, someone I've worked with (and who shared with me the elephant analogy) commented that top 100 ASX companies work with her because she has already worked with 20 of them, including 5 in the top 10. If these companies are happy to work with her, often more than once, other companies (the leaders in them) are following this endorsement.

Informal ingredients

The informal ingredients are perhaps the ones we need to be attuned to but they are much harder to get a reading on.

Over time, the accumulated observation of your words and actions forms the basis of what people say about you. Opinions, rumour and gossip can gain traction very quickly, and nowadays it can also be very public. Once started, rumour and gossip are almost impossible to stop, even if factually incorrect.

People are more likely to share negative feedback, even without being asked. Someone who has had a bad restaurant experience will tell 10 people, and someone who has had a good experience, just one or two.

It's important to understand that some opinions count more than others. And just whose opinion matters more to you will depend on what your career or profession is, how visible you are in your role (or want to be), who you regard as important in your sphere, and how much you value the opinions of your colleagues, friends and family, and perhaps even public opinion.

HOW BEHAVIOUR AND PERCEPTIONS WORK TOGETHER

You are responsible for your behaviours, but not how others perceive them.

Below I share a diagram that illustrates how I see behaviour and perceptions working together. Your behaviour, in terms of your *actions* and *values*, is what you can control. The *perceptible reality* is what others 'see' you as. When these are aligned, you are in the best space in terms of your reputation (in the centre). Here your reputation is as a trusted, relevant and authentic person. As such, you can have the impact on the areas of your work, family, community and country that you wish.

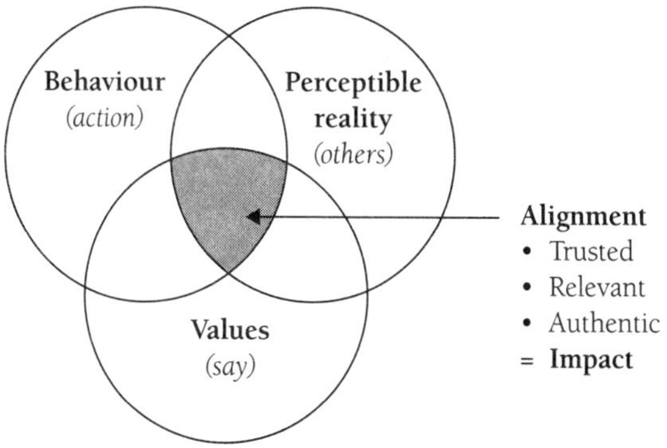

If your actions and words are *not* aligned, the perceptible reality about you is either confused or negative. Your reputation is mixed and you are regarded as unreliable in some areas and reliable in others, but people are unsure of which 'you' they are going to get.

This goes for brands as well. In an article about what to expect in brand experience in 2019, the team at The Prophet noted that 75% of the 300,000 people they interviewed wanted brands to make more of a contribution to their wellbeing and quality of life. More importantly, the 2019 Edelman Trust Barometer shows that trust in American companies fell again to just 50%, down from 55% in the prior year and 61% in 2014.[9]

Separately, The Prophet team noted that, 'Millennial attacks against "fake wokeness" and the brands that use it are swift and effective, whether it's Pepsi appropriating Black Lives Matter, Audi's faux concern about pay equity or Dodge co-opting Martin Luther King Jr … if you're going to brag about helping girls code or being an eco-warrior, you better be ready to prove it.'[10]

'Fake wokeness' lacks authenticity. It's when actions and words don't add up; the brand is simply not being authentic and levels of trust (and therefore purchases) decline. If the brand doesn't reassess what it's doing and saying and make sure they're aligned, they'll become less relevant and, ultimately, stranded.

Take CPA Australia. The brand has been significantly damaged due to the actions of its board and former CEO. It's still in the process of rebuilding its brand, and it will take time.

---

9 https://www.edelman.com/sites/g/files/aatuss191/files/2019-01/2019_Edelman_Trust_Barometer_Executive_Summary.pdf

10 http://www.prophet.com. 'Brand and Experience: What to expect in 2019'.

THE POWER OF SOCIAL MEDIA

Here are a couple of brand disasters that show the power of social media.

In 2008, the band Sons of Maxwell flew from Chicago to Nebraska with United Airlines, and a $3500 guitar labelled fragile was damaged during the journey. Singer David Carroll communicated with the airline over nine months, but no compensation was offered and United refused to accept responsibility.

Frustrated, Carroll and his band wrote a song documenting the experience and posted it to YouTube, where it has been viewed over 19 million times. The song is called *United Breaks Guitars*. The PR train wreck prompted the airline to eventually offer to replace the instrument, but the damage had been done.[11]

In late 2011, after months of negative publicity stemming from industrial disputes that resulted in the grounding of the Qantas fleet, their PR team sent out a call for luxury flying experiences. #QantasLuxury was promoted as a chance to win first-class cabin pyjamas for those using the hashtag. But Qantas demonstrated a lack of appreciation for how social media works, and the hashtag was hijacked. These are some of the responses: '#QantasLuxury – when the passengers arrive before the couriers delivering the lockout notices do', and, '#QantasLuxury – giving yourself a pay rise whilst grounding your whole airline and taking local jobs offshore'.[12]

And, more recently, the actions of Rugby Australia against Israel Folau and his social media posts have damaged both the sporting code's brand and that of the individual. Sportswear company ASICS

---

11 https://www.zdnet.com/pictures/10-brands-damaged-by-social-media-disasters/9/

12 https://www.smh.com.au/business/small-business/australias-biggest-pr-disasters-20130926-2ugli.html

dumped Folau after Rugby Australia terminated his contract, while fans have been polarised and other sponsors tried to stay out of the ensuing ruck. The issue gained national and international attention, with Folau launching legal proceedings against Rugby Australia through the Fair Work Commission, only for a confidential settlement to be reached in December 2019. The matter continues to damage both brands, with Folau's recent signing to the European Super League Club Catalans Dragons attracting a significant backlash. No winners there at all.

SO WHAT VALUES AND ACTIONS ARE A GOOD STARTING POINT?

> *'You can't build a reputation on what you are going to do.'*
> – Henry Ford

I've outlined below in no specific order 11 values and actions that are a good starting point when you are trying to establish and maintain 'brand you'. You may well have others. Write your own list of what's important to you, and how you are going to demonstrate this.

1. Stand by your word

Do what you say you're going to do and say what you mean. Be reliable and dependable; this is how you build trust and gain more responsibility.

2. Help others realise their potential

Go out of your way to help others reach their goals. Being reputable goes beyond a concern for yourself and your own advancement. Foster a mindset of helping other people.

3. Exceed expectations

Go a step (or two) beyond what is expected. The actions of someone who goes above and beyond will be noticed: they stand out as a positive role model for everyone.

4. Show integrity in action

Do what's right. Values matter. Operate with integrity at all times. If you wouldn't buy the product or service you are selling, don't sell it. If you see the wrong thing happening, do something to prevent it happening or happening again.

5. Be consistent and have tenacity

You need to show the same great qualities you have to everyone you meet. When your behaviour is steady and reliable, your actions become predictable. Have consistent and relentless focus on performance.

6. Get engaged with your community

Being engaged means getting to know people, giving back your time and resources, and being available.

7. Show thoughtfulness in your actions

Think before you act. Are you proud of who you are, what you say and what you do? Ask yourself: 'Is what I'm doing worthy of my best self?'

8. Own accountability

Be honest about your mistakes and failures. Accept responsibility for your actions. If you wouldn't be proud to see your words or actions in a newspaper headline, don't say them or do them. If things go wrong despite your best intentions, face the consequences with an apology and your plan to do better.

9. Show compassion in action

Show you care about other people. It's important to find ways to recognise and support other people, whoever they are. Be aware of other people's needs and help without expectation of a 'return'. Thank them, recognise them and be respectful.

10. Look the part

Be sure to dress for the reputation you are working to build. First impressions count, and people will make judgements about the way you look, write, post, appear on social media and interact. Your body language tells people a lot about what you think about yourself and what you think about them.

11. Create visibility and connections

You have to ensure people notice you, that they see your performance. Reputations don't work very well in isolation, they need a network of supporters, fans and advocates to spread the word. Getting others to sing your praises is far more effective than you trying to do it yourself. It's also good to associate with others who have strong reputations that complement your own.

> *'We judge ourselves by what we feel capable of doing, while others judge us by what we have already done.'* – Henry Wadsworth Longfellow

4 Building valuable connections and networks

Considering who you invest time in developing deep relationships with has to be based on your core values, passions and beliefs. Anything less than this will render you at best inconsistent in your actions and, at worst, someone who is disloyal.

None of us can predict what the future holds in our business and personal lives. But all of us have a choice about who we associate with, how much time, effort and energy we put into these relationships, and the longevity of these. The question we're exploring here is who and how we identify, develop and nurture the business and community networks we need to grow our relevance and therefore ability to lead in the areas we choose.

THE CHANGING WORK ENVIRONMENT

One of the actions I mentioned at the end of the previous chapter was that building connections is an important component in growing your reputation. This is even more essential in a business environment, with AI and automation changing the way in which some work is undertaken in whole or in part, the move towards the gig economy for professionals and executives, and shorter tenures in executive and management roles.

Of course, depending on where you are in your career journey, the breadth and depth of your networks will vary. The key points here though are it's important to recognise that you need to start building networks early, they need to be varied (not just your workplace or your industry), you need to invest time and possibly money to start and build them, and you need to be actively engaging with your networks, giving back as well as seeking support and advice.

You also need to be aware of the changing nature of the workplace, even in professions where traditionally career paths, tenures and roles have been more stable. Worldwide, the trend is for companies and professional firms to seek specialists not generalists, to contract executives for specific projects or skill sets. Welcome to the world of the interim executive – it's coming to a company or organisation that you're working in now.

In 2019, leading executive recruitment company Watermark International published its annual management survey and noted the following trends:

- The profile of interim executives is shifting, with 'portfolio working' seen as a legitimate career choice.
- For those choosing this option, networking is a critical factor in their success, as is the ability of an executive to promote their 'superpowers' effectively.
- Companies who are 'borrowing' interim executive talent are doing so at the General Manager and Head of Department level.

Interestingly, 71% of survey respondents said that prior job contacts were the best way of gaining work, with 58% saying their own network was important.[1]

Another interesting component to the interim executive trend is that industry knowledge is less critical than specialist business transformation, digital transformation and cultural change knowledge.

Understanding how the business world is changing is critical if you are to select and develop strong networks that will be useful to you, and who you can be useful for over time. Strong connections within your industry sector and outside it will give you a wider network of people who can help you navigate the changing business environment, move industry sectors or secure exposure to or the opportunity for new leadership roles.

THE DIFFERENCE BETWEEN CONNECTING AND A NETWORK

Linking on social media platforms is an important, if not essential, part of developing a network, whatever age or stage you are in your career.

In 2009 one of Australia's leading social media commentators, Iggy Pintado, published a book titled *The Connection Generation*. Iggy was way ahead of his time. In 2013, when most business executives had not even heard of LinkedIn and thought social media was for children not those seeking a career in business or the professions, Iggy was ranked #3 most connected Australian on LinkedIn and #88 globally.[2]

---

1 Watermark Interim Management Survey 2019.

2 http://www.iggypintado.com.au

His book is a fascinating study of how connectedness affects our place in society and business, and the challenges and opportunities this compelling development presents.

As of March 2020, LinkedIn has:

- 9.8 million members in Australia
- 1.5 million members in New Zealand
- 26.2 million members in the UK
- 158.6 million members in the US
- 675 million members worldwide.[3]

As one of my LinkedIn connections commented recently, 'Still think LinkedIn isn't worth your valuable time?'

A long-standing colleague of mine had to cajole her 24-year-old son who is still at university to update his LinkedIn profile, as he wanted to secure some part-time work. Initially, her son was resistant. LinkedIn was for 'older people' (like his mum), not him. But within three weeks of updating his profile, including getting a professional photo taken, he had secured two offers of part-time, paid work. This for a maths/physics student.

If you're a student, LinkedIn is the ideal way for you to start developing your own network.

If you are in a professional firm, working up the executive ladder in a larger corporate or heading out the other end of a corporate career, LinkedIn would have to be one of the most powerful ways for you to develop your public profile and grow your connections. To do this, you need to be very clear about 'brand you', and you need to know how to utilise LinkedIn.

---

3 Lynnaire Johnston, https://www.linkedin.com/in/lynnairejohnston/

LinkedIn and other social media platforms, as well as industry associations and not-for-profit organisations, provide you the opportunity to connect. You can develop a network with people across these areas but it's not a given, and connecting is not the same as building a strong, committed network of trusted people. Building up a close network of trusted advisers, mentors, coaches and supporters take years, sometimes decades to develop. These are the professional relationships that are long term, respectful, open, honest, reciprocal and highly rewarding for both parties.

HOW TO DEVELOP YOUR NETWORK AND WHO TO INCLUDE

Who you are linked to (people and companies) matters in terms of your reputation and relevance over the long term. I say 'the long term' because who you attach yourself to in the short term may not be the best decision for you in the long term, even if the money or status looks compelling right now. This is when the clarity about your values 'hits the road'.

When thinking about who you want to develop a network with, you need to identify those individuals who are involved with and leading the causes you are passionate about. Your passions and purpose might be business or career orientated or community orientated, or a combination of both. Equally, you might admire a leader in another area altogether and decide their values and passion are something you want to become part of.

The most important part of choosing who or which organisations you want to grow a network with is how they match up with your values and passion. To develop a deep network of respect and mutual engagement and support takes a long time, and you're only going to add value to a network over time if you're deeply committed to it. If you're not, sporadic interest will be seen for what it is: superficial. Your actions won't match up with your words.

For example, George Calombaris, the celebrity chef and *MasterChef* judge and director of Made Establishment Group with 12 high-profile restaurants, underpaid the workers in his restaurants for several years by $7.8 million. He was fined by the Fair Work Ombudsman for this, and paid back $7.83 million in minimum award rates, penalty rates, overtime loading, casual rates, split shift rates and more.[4]

Would you eat at one of his restaurants if you had the choice? I wouldn't. No matter how good his food is, those values don't match mine. And, as it turned out many others had the same view as in early February 2020 an administrator was appointed to Calombaris's Made Establishment.

It's getting harder for me to eat out as several other celebrity chefs have been found to be operating in the same way, underpaying some of the hardest workers: their kitchen staff, wait staff and cleaners, including a restaurant linked with Heston Blumenthal (Dinner by Heston) and Neil Perry of Rockpool Dining Group.[5] Like Calombaris, Dinner by Heston was also placed into administration in early 2020 owing some $4.5 million to its workers.[6]

An interesting dynamic to George's denouement was that systemic underpayments of employees by some of Australia's major companies and law firms to the level of hundreds of millions of

---

4 https://www.watoday.com.au/national/victoria/george-calombaris-underpayment-scandal-calls-for-celebrity-to-be-sacked-from-masterchef-20190718-p528dj.html

5 https://www.stuff.co.nz/business/world/116344841/the-celebrity-chefs-who-have-been-busted-for-underpaying-staff

6 https://www.abc.net.au/news/2020-02-04/dinner-by-heston-underpaid-staff-by-more-than-4-million-dollars/11928746

dollars made Calombaris's transgression seem minor in comparison and to a degree diminished the impact on his reputation.[7]

Take another example, that of the brand of Belle Gibson and the Whole Pantry App, book, and social media presence that I've mentioned before. Penguin Random House, Apple and other respected brands were tarnished by their association with her. Brands pulled their projects based on her story when it was uncovered that it was untrue. Penguin Random House and Apple had sound business reasons for linking with her, but did not explore deep enough into the 'facts' around her.

Let's explore another example. Would you consider seeking out Clive Palmer as a business mentor or business associate? You may well say yes, and that's your prerogative. However, it would be remiss at best and cavalier at worst not to research and understand how he does business and assess whether his values and approach align with yours.

On the opposite side, Roger Federer has a terrific reputation and he's linked with brands that are aligned with his values and actions (clearly they think so, too), such as Rolex, Mercedes-Benz, Credit Suisse, Uniqlo, Moët & Chandon and Rimowa.[8] In Australia, Atlassian has developed a strong reputation for its culture and values. People want to work for the company because of these, and are proud to say they work for this company. Having pride in who you work with is the ultimate goal for many people, and it means being aware of the external dynamics of the company and how they act and are perceived.

---

7 https://www.abc.net.au/news/2019-10-30/woolworths-underpays-5700-staff-up-to-300-million-dollars/11652656

8 https://www.rogerfederer.com/index.php/sponsors

And if you think perceptions don't count, just look at the challenges Huawei is facing around the globe trying to sell its technology. The US and Australia have both banned the company from bidding for government contracts due to concerns around national security risks.

NETWORKS ARE DYNAMIC

As with everything else in life, the networks you build in and across business and the wider community are constantly changing. Given the average tenure for a CEO in the US is 5 years[9] and Australia is 5.5 years,[10] and executive-level roles are probably less, a critical factor for anyone in business, at whatever level they are at, is to focus less on the role someone has and instead focus on their values and relevance.

Companies are taken over, taken out, restructured, privatised, floated, corporatised and collapse every day. New companies are formed, grow, IPO, soar and keep soaring. Some companies continue for generations, like the company I'm connected with, but private and family businesses have become increasingly focused on performance rather than genetics. And this 'performance and accountability' focus applies to community organisations, not-for-profits and even your family in a way.

YOUR VALUES AND YOUR NETWORK

The values I hold close to me and espouse come from my parents and their values about what was right and what was wrong and learning the difference between the extremes.

---

9 https://corpgov.law.harvard.edu/2018/02/12/ceo-tenure-rates/

10 https://www.afr.com/leadership/ceo-tenure-hits-fiveyear-high-pwc-finds-20161205-gt3wmy

I have endeavoured to continue learning and strengthen my understanding of what are the appropriate values for every aspect of my life, whether it is family, business or community. I have made it part of my DNA, and tried to impart this to my sons. In business it was not difficult as CEO to embed my values, however at times I was accused of being unbalanced and skewed, and at other times as being more focused on *values* than *value*. I have been faced with many situations where I've had to make choices that impact on my values and beliefs. When that decision is made, even today, I feel empowered and stronger, knowing I have elected the high moral ground that others struggle to take or see. Fairness and consistency, for me, are just as important as respect, excellence and integrity.

When I was growing up I wanted to be liked, however as I have grown older it is respect for my values and views I hold more dearly, and this translates into reputation and a strong positioning of who I am and my relevance in many areas where trust, credibility and dependability are paramount.

Throughout your life, if you want to maintain your relevance and reputation, you need to have awareness of what's happening in the environments you are operating in, when and why. For example, a person may be popular, have a bestselling product or service, and you might seek to be associated with them. However, popularity is a fickle thing, and when the popularity or trend wanes or, worse still, is damaged, what does this mean for you? This applies to a brand, a company, a person – your immediate boss, your CEO, your friend, your mentor.

Recognise you need to develop strong and deep networks. Be selective about who you seek to develop these relationships with. Your reputation and relevance at various points in time will determine whether they want to engage you.

Edward Kennedy at Bobby Kennedy's funeral said:

> *My brother need not be idealized, or enlarged in death beyond what he was in life; to be remembered simply as a good and decent man, who saw wrong and tried to right it, saw suffering and tried to heal it, saw war and tried to stop it.*

What an honour to be remembered this way.

WHEN YOUR VALUES ARE TESTED

It's the scenario we will all face. Someone in our close network hits the headlines for all the wrong reasons. You're close to them as a business partner, supplier, sponsor, a colleague, friend or family member. Something happens and they become a liability for you or your business. What do you do? How do you deal with it, communicate it and manage it?

Do you stand by this person or not?

This will be one of the toughest decisions you'll ever have to make, and throughout your business and personal life you will have to make these decisions a number of times. A close colleague, mentor, friend today might be a liability tomorrow. The choices you make are critical at both a personal and professional level. You might have conflicting emotions, loyalties and concerns about your own reputation and financial security.

Implication by association is a reality.

The one thing that is absolute is that not making choices is a critical failure. Doing nothing is *not* an option. You'll have to make decisions and act on them. And there are always consequences.

If you are clear about your values and have articulated these throughout your networks by your actions and behaviour, when you are faced with this challenge you'll be in a much stronger and clearer place to make decisions that are aligned to your values and to communicate your position to those who are impacted by your decision.

Part II

THE RELEVANCE JOURNEY

5 Relevance over time

VOLATILITY, UNCERTAINTY, COMPLEXITY AND AMBIGUITY

Prior to 2020 there was wide acknowledgment that we were living in a rapidly evolving business environment of volatility, uncertainty, complexity and ambiguity (VUCA). As of March 2020 the COVID-19 pandemic has changed *everything* for *everyone*. Uncertainty and volatility are primary drivers now and in the near future. The democratisation of information (thanks to Google and others) and the ever-growing interconnectedness of everyone through AI and data (sometimes with our permission but often without it) is also transforming business models. Algorithms push us information, products and services they think we might be interested in based on online purchases, browsing patterns and in some cases eye movements across the screen and in supermarkets. Information is fed to us that supports our world view, and we have to work hard to not believe the feedback loop that the rest of the world 'sees' the world as we do … it's simply that if we're too lazy to look for ourselves the algorithms are more than happy to take advantage of this.

Combined with this is the increasing shift towards gig work, not just at the blue-collar levels of business but, more and more, in middle and senior management, the professions and across education, health and social services.

What's all this got to do with relevance?

Everything.

Working out who to trust and how we can be regarded as trustworthy in such a complex environment is a real challenge. Understanding what our own values are and living these in an authentic way is also a challenge. Individuals, especially leaders, are being called on to articulate their values, to earn the trust of their colleagues and communities. People, commentators, the media and even your family and friends have more avenues and opportunity to 'see' just who you are.

And there's more and more of an expectation that you need to be able and ready to articulate who you are, your brand.

One example of the challenges leaders are facing today is Larry Fink, CEO of BlackRock, the world's largest investment management company with over US$6 trillion under management. In January 2019 Fink announced that his company would change its hiring policies and potentially its compensation structure to advance diversity and ensure that five years from now the company was not just a 'bunch of white men'. This on the back of an earlier statement that companies needed to embrace a purpose beyond profit maximisation.

There were numerous critics of these policies and statements, mostly along the lines that it is not the role of a CEO of a public company to use his position to advance a personal agenda and that company money should not be used to further a goal that may not create economic returns.

Supporters, however, pointed out that business leaders needed to stop pretending that business somehow exists in a vacuum that neither affects nor depends on the wellbeing of society.[1] Committing to a purpose and having a positive social impact is increasingly central to good management and shareholder value and there's research to back this up.[2]

Whether you agree with the critics or supporters of Fink, you need to have a viewpoint, take a position, act, present and defend it. Your values, actions and what you say will determine how others view you, trust you and support you … in short, your relevance and impact.

If you say one thing and do another, the misalignment between what you say and do will lead to uncertainty about who you are and what you really stand for. The level of trust in you as a leader, and potentially your company, will decline and you'll have less impact. Just look at what happened to Volkswagen over its emissions tests, Valeant Pharmaceuticals when it excessively raised prices on its drugs, AMP when it kept taking fees from dead people, and many of the banks charging for advice that was never delivered.

Counter to these examples, look at the lead that numerous Australian companies took in the marriage equality referendum held in 2018. Coca-Cola joined hundreds of other businesses and organisations – including Apple, Qantas, Westpac, Target, Cricket Australia, NRL and AFL – supporting the 'yes' campaign. Qantas CEO Alan Joyce was particularly vocal and faced many of the same

1 'The Backlash to Larry Fink's Letter', Mark Kramer, *HBR*, 31 January 2019.

2 https://www.hbs.edu/faculty/Pages/item.aspx?num=54523

criticisms that Larry Fink did. Coca-Cola even changed its iconic sign at the top of Kings Cross, replacing the red logo with rainbow colours.[3]

Similarly, many Australian business leaders have come out strongly in support of the School Strike for Climate, despite the Prime Minister's comments that he thinks business is embarking on too many activist causes. Atlassian was very vocal, as was Tim Reed (the outgoing CEO of MYOB), the Business Council of Australia, and some 3100-plus businesses that supported the 'This is Not Business as Usual' campaign in support of the strike.[4]

In addition, the Committee for the Development of Australia (CEDA) undertook a nationwide poll of 3000 people and 70% of them agreed large companies should place equal importance on economic, environmental and social performance, and more than three-quarters supported business leaders speaking out on issues of national importance.[5]

Again, whatever your position on each issue, you need to take a stand if you are a leader of a company or of a small team within a company or organisation. In a world where trust is harder to earn, where people are less trusting of what they see and read, your values, actions and words are more critical than ever in developing, maintaining and articulating brand you … of being a trusted person with relevance and impact.

---

3 https://www.news.com.au/lifestyle/food/drink/cocacola-cans-and-iconic-sydney-billboard-to-change-to-rainbow-colours-in-support-of-marriage-equality/news-story/d0d44e848b4aa6cacfa57117bd492ca6

4 https://www.notbusinessasusual.co

5 https://www.ceda.com.au/News-and-analysis/Media-releases/CEDA-national-poll-Australians-expect-more-from-business-than-just-profits

YOUR RELEVANCE CONSTANTLY CHANGES

Relevance, like most things in life, is a dynamic concept. Your relevance changes over time and across different groups within your life over time. It evolves and is shaped as you grow up, is shaped by circumstances, events and your actions – or inaction.

Your relevance at a point in time and over time are impacted by events, associations and actions within your control and outside it. In the age of social media your actions at a younger age can and probably will revisit you in later life. We don't have to look too far to see this in action. In the 2019 Federal Election, seven candidates were forced to withdraw within the first three weeks of the election, some for social media posts they had uploaded several years in the past. These included Jeremy Hearn for anti-Muslim comments, Luke Creasey for sharing jokes about rape seven years previously, Jessica Whelan for anti-Muslim comments, and Peter Killin for homophobic remarks. And then we saw the demise of NSW Opposition Leader Michael Daley, whose comments about Asians taking local jobs was shared on social media and ended his career.

After Luke Creasey's posts became public, he noted that, 'This is a really important lesson for young people that your social media footprint will follow you.' The same article also quoted an unnamed operator: 'You have to assume everything is on the record. If you're not prepared to stand by it for the rest of your life, don't say it.'[6]

The changing nature and scope of relevance over time is why it's important for you to deeply understand your values and how your actions align, or otherwise, with these. Virtually no one comes to their values accidentally, and knowing your values is not

---

6 https://www.smh.com.au/federal-election-2019/candidates-skittled-as-political-dirt-units-enter-overdrive-in-the-social-media-era-20190503-p51jxw.html

enough. If your values aren't tied to specific behaviours they become empty words.

MY RELEVANCE IMPACT

I've developed a model of My Relevance Impact (MyRI) based on over 40 years in the FMCG (fast-moving consumer goods) branding area, alongside decades of working in and observing how personal branding has developed and become a critical part in competing for influence and impact.

I developed the MyRI to give you a basis to help you understand where you are in terms of your relevance, where you want to be and how you can move from one to the other so you can increase your impact.

There are many organisations in product and service brand work that are experienced and reputable in measuring brands and their impact and relevance. One of the most recognisable is Interbrand, who pioneered brand valuation in 1988. While they are focused on business brands, it's useful to understand their criteria, some of which transfer across to personal branding – other parts do not.

On their website, Interbrand states that:

> *We have a deep understanding of the impact a strong brand has on key stakeholder groups that influence the growth of your business, namely (current and prospective) customers, employees, and investors. Strong brands influence customer choice and create loyalty; attract, retain, and motivate talent; and lower the cost of financing.*[7]

---

7 https://www.interbrand.com

They use three key components in all their brand valuations:

- an analysis of the financial performance of the branded products or services
- the role the brand plays in purchase decisions
- the brand's competitive strength.

While the first two components can be morphed across to the personal branding space, it's the third – the brand's competitive strength – where the most synergy lies. Interbrand lists 10 brand strengths. I've put these in the left-hand column below. In the right-hand column I've reinterpreted them for personal branding.

Interbrand strengths for business brands	Brand you
Internal	
Clarity	Knowing your values, knowing your 'audience' and what matters to them.
Commitment	Reliable, hardworking, stepping up. What's your passion and how does this manifest itself?
Governance	Your internal compass. Self-assessment and external feedback if unsure.
Responsiveness	An ability to evolve in response to where you are in your life, changes in society, to challenges and opportunities.

Interbrand strengths for business brands	Brand you
External	
Authenticity	A defined story and value set that is communicated clearly and consistently.
Relevance	Fit with the needs, desires and outcomes of specific groups in time and over time.
Differentiation	What makes you different, stand out? What are you known for? How well do you compete in your area?
Consistency	Values and behaviours are aligned. You do as you say.
Presence	What others say about you, how often and in what context. Are you leading or following?
Engagement	How often and who engages you and how do they identify with you? What level of exposure do you have in your chosen fields?

I've morphed the business brand model, which is rightly focused on the economic measurement of a brand's value. While our own personal brand does have some impact at an economic level (what we can earn or charge for), it's not the primary factor in understanding personal branding and relevance impact. So much of our relevance and impact is not within our control and is often not factually based.

There are three key components to our MyRI model (shown in the following image):

1. Values.
2. Behaviour.
3. Perceptible reality (what others think of us either from first-hand experience or, more often than not, second-, third- or fourth-hand commentary).

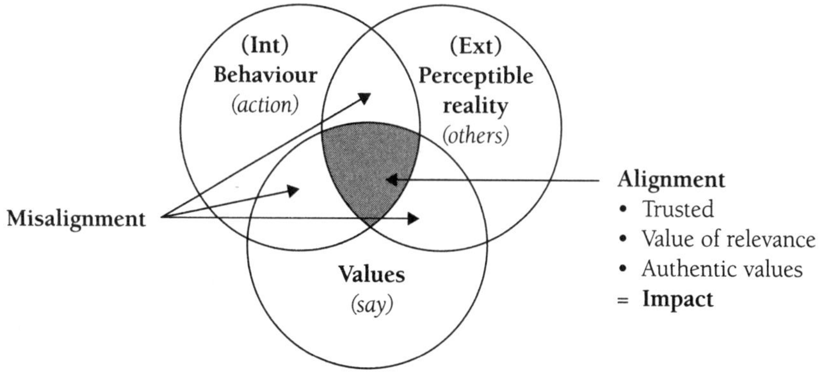

If all three are in complete alignment, the middle space, you have the maximum opportunity to have impact in whatever it is you choose to do. Whether you do or not is another discussion altogether.

When your words, actions and perceptions of others are in alignment you are trusted, your values are clear, you are regarded as authentic and therefore can make a larger impact as others will follow you.

Where your values and behaviours are aligned but others don't perceive that they are, your relevance and impact are lower.

Where your behaviours and others' perceptions of them don't match your values, you're compromised, something that for most people is not sustainable over time. You risk censure from others, the community and the law.

Where your values and behaviour don't align, the external perception of you is confused at best and negative at worst; think Tiger Woods in sport, Ken Henry in the Banking Royal Commission, FIFA and Sepp Blatter, the IOC and Juan Antonio Samaranch.

If they do align and they are negative (think Nick Kyrgios in sport, Bill Clinton, Christopher Skase) your impact and relevance are compromised.

Alan Joyce, CEO of Qantas, provides an interesting example of his personal interest and how he has linked with community engagement and the customer. Prostate cancer affected Alan, and he chose to share his diagnosis and increase awareness of the disease with a cause-related marketing program. The broader community, I believe, were accepting of the initiative.

Joyce also took a prominent role in the gay marriage debate and referendum. As an openly gay man and leading CEO, he used his role to promote the yes vote to the wider community. In my view, this damaged his image with a section of the Australian community as he was seen as imposing his opinion and influence on Qantas's customers and the wider community.

THE FOUR RELEVANCE STAGES

Linked with this model is the need to understand where you are in your life and how this impacts on your relevance to the primary target audiences at each of these stages.

I've broken down the relevance journey into four key stages to reflect (approximately) the journey from childhood/adolescence to early adulthood, professional maturity and wisdom/retirement. Of course, everyone charts their own journey and there will always be outliers, the exception to the rule. I've used these broad categories to help describe the dynamics of relevance and key stages in most people's lives and especially those in business and the professions:

1. Childhood and adolescence (0 to 20)
2. Early adulthood (early career: 20s to 30s)
3. Professional maturity (prime career: 30s to mid 50s)
4. Wisdom and retirement (mid 50s onwards).

I've also overlaid in the following image what I consider the four main areas of relevance for most people: family, work, community, country.

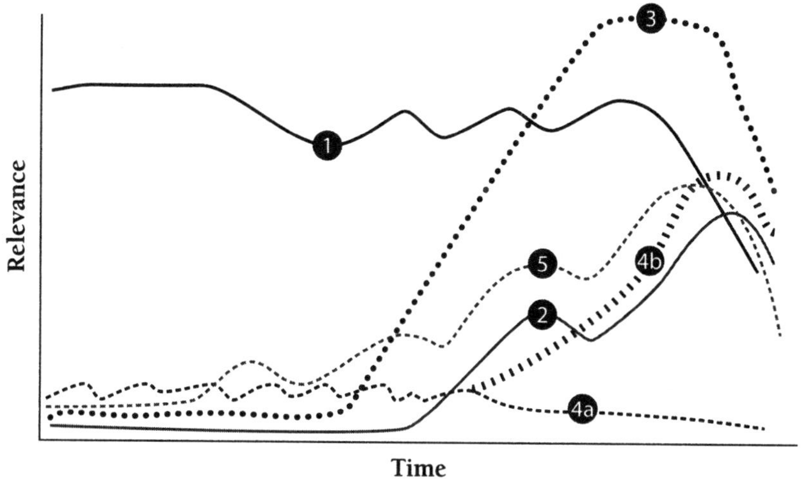

Different pathways depending on:

1. Family 1
2. Family 2 (your own)
3. Business

4a. Community (not active)
4b. Community (active)
5. Country (possible)

Clearly, everyone's journey is different in terms of actual timing. What I'm trying to show is that:

- it is a journey
- relevance changes over time across the different areas
- there might be times when you have to make clear decisions about where and how you are going to be most relevant; this may require trade-offs, so you had better be clear about your purpose and impact.

This assumes you are clear on your values and outside influences are benign, but that's mostly not the reality.

* * *

In the following chapters I'll share with you my insights about where you are at on the relevance journey, and what you can do to proactively manage 'brand you' to develop and then build on your relevance.

By following this relevance journey you'll gain a better understanding of where you're at now, be better equipped to make positive and proactive decisions about what impact you want to have and where, gain insights into your own values and beliefs, and understand how you 'walk the talk' every day.

6 Childhood and adolescence (0 to 20)

For most of us our childhood and adolescence is not a period where we spend much, if any, time thinking about our personal brand, unless of course you are a child or teen sports star, musician, writer, model, in a boy or girl band or otherwise a public figure early in life.

From the time they are born through to around 15 to 16 years old, children are mostly not conscious of the dynamics of a personal brand and relevance. Most are highly relevant to their immediate family and close extended family. As you develop friendships outside the family, friends become more or less relevant over time. You might have a shifting number of friends and develop a few longer term friendships.

Depending on your upbringing and interests, you might also start developing relevance in community groups and sporting groups. Again, your relevance for these groups will probably change over time as you become more or less involved.

So, as you're growing up, your relevance to family stays strong while relevance to others shifts. Throughout this period though you are developing a personal brand. Initially you'll be unaware of this, but it is happening. And, for young people these days, with so many social media platforms on offer, there's a high likelihood they've been actively working on their personal brand and relevance without really thinking about it.

As you move through secondary school you might become more and more aware that you have a brand, and that everyone has one, whether they like it or not. The fact is that when people think of you – your family, friends, teachers, teammates and club members – they have some kind of impression in their minds about who you are and what you stand for.

So, the question is, is your personal brand a good one or not? And a follow-up question is, do you care, or not?

HOW DO OTHERS SEE YOU?

Again, younger people tend not to think about this too deeply; they're more focused on how they look rather than who they are, their values and how they are perceived. Also, young people are still working through what their values are, as they've mostly taken on those of their parents. It's not till our later teens and 20s when we start to formulate our own core beliefs and make decisions based on these.

Some, even at a young age, are firm in their beliefs, values and behaviours and are prepared to live by them, choosing their friends and groups based on these.

Sometimes events act as a catalyst for clear decision making about values and actions. Take the experience of Malala Yousafzai.

Malala was born in 1997 in Pakistan. Her father was a teacher and taught girls and boys. In 2008 the Taliban stopped girls attending school; in 2012 Malala spoke out against this. As a result, she was targeted and was shot in the head. She was treated in England, and her family also moved there.

She has fully recovered, and has become an activist for the right for girls to go to school. In her own words:

> *It was then I knew I had a choice. I could live a quiet life or I could make the most of this new life I had been given. I was determined to fight until every girl could go to school.*[1]

In recognition of the work of her foundation, she was awarded the Nobel Peace Prize in 2014 at the age of 17, the youngest recipient ever.

At the other end of the spectrum we have Taylor Swift, who at the age of 14 moved to Tennessee to pursue a career in country music. She signed with label Big Machine Records and became the youngest artist signed by the Sony/ATV Music House. One of the bestselling artists of all time, she has used her power to take on Spotify and Apple Music over music royalty payments.

And then there's:

- sports stars such as Ian Thorpe – at 14, the youngest ever male individual world champion
- politicians – at 20, Wyatt Roy was the youngest ever Australian elected to Parliament
- entrepreneurs – at 12, Bella Tipping started Kidzcationz in 2015.

---

1 https://www.malala.org/malalas-story

How others see you also means you have to be aware of how you present yourself in person and online. Everyone has tremendous potential, but because of the way many people are perceived by others, the way other people look at, value, think and talk about them, they never get a chance to use that potential, to be relevant and have impact.

Your appearance matters.

Your attitude is vital.

Your character is of paramount importance.

Keep your promises. Unmet expectations are the arch enemy of any relationship, and 'brand you' as a person is determined in large part by whether you consistently deliver on your promises.

Do you keep your word? Do you follow up? Do your words and actions match with the image you want to create; that is, with the values, qualities and attributes you claim as your own? And when you make a mistake, and we all do, do you own up to it, take corrective action, resolve to get back on track and learn from the experience?

Your overall behaviour strongly influences the impressions others have of you. Be punctual for meetings and appointments. Be absolutely reliable, always keep to your word and your commitments.

As to whether you care or not, the reality is that you need to if you want to stand out, prosper and make an impact in the areas that matter to you.

STANDING OUT

Tom Peters, who wrote *In Search of Excellence*, wrote a great piece about personal branding way back in 1997. If you haven't read it you should, as it's as relevant and actionable today as it was over

20 years ago. One thing he wrote that's particularly relevant for younger people when starting to think about your own personal brand was:

> *Regardless of age, regardless of position, regardless of the business we happen to be in, all of us need to understand the importance of branding. We are CEOs of our own companies: Me Inc. To be in business today, our most important job is to be head marketer for the brand called You. It's that simple – and that hard. And that inescapable.*[2]

Your personal branding and relevance are already at work in your early and late teens. How people perceive you and your relevance to them determines whether they're connected with you, following you, will return your messages, like your Insta images … everything.

Once you understand this, you might then look at *how* and *what* you are sharing so that it represents who you are, your values, behaviours and passions. And if there's a disconnect between these, you need to start working out what has to change … and soon. You can do this in your teens and while you're at university, and if you do, you'll be way ahead of the rest of your cohort … which can make a significant difference when you're heading into the workforce or setting up your own business in your early 20s.

Tom Peters also provides some great advice about how to do this, and I've summarised it:

1. What is it that makes me different from others (in 15 words or less)?
2. What are my values?

---

2 https://www.fastcompany.com/28905/brand-called-you?page=0,0

3. What are qualities and characteristics that make me distinctive from my peer group?
4. What do I do that adds remarkable, measurable, distinguished, distinctive value?
5. What do I want to be famous for?

Once you've worked through these, you then have to find ways to be visible to the people you want to recognise you … well, be relevant to.

How do you do this? At this early stage in your life you volunteer for projects, you join specific groups and take on different levels of responsibility and maybe leadership roles, *and* you write about them so what you're doing is visible. Don't wait for someone to notice you – chances are they won't. If you're not comfortable doing this, seek some advice from someone you trust.

Social media can come back to haunt you

As I mentioned in the introduction to this section, the world is littered with would-be leaders or people who wanted to be a leader in their field only to come unstuck because of social media images and posts they authored or uploaded years ago, and we're talking about people who did not grow up digital natives.

If you're born after 2000, you've known social media your whole life, and it'll know you extremely well by the time you are in your late teens.

I am all for encouraging younger people to take control of their brand and utilise the online world to be visible to increase their relevance, but you need to think about what you are posting and sharing on what platform, and the fact that once it's posted it's very hard to remove and that your future employers, business partners, colleagues and employees may well be looking at your posts 15, 20 and 30 years down the track. Again, don't post anything you wouldn't want to read about or look at on the front page of your daily newspaper.

MENTORS

It's also never too early to find a mentor – in fact, you might have two or three. Throughout my life, many people have helped me on my way; some have been mentors and others friends or acquaintances who have been around at a difficult time. Mentors have stuck with me and followed up with me on my progress and development of individual pursuits. Some mentor relationships started off as an informal introduction to provide assistance for a particular goal I was aiming to achieve. Others came into my life and I connected with them so well that a longer term relationship formed.

In my early years my long-time athletics trainer Jack Pross was a disciplinarian who stood by me in highs and lows of competitive sport, and was there to give me tough advice related to athletics and also on life. Jack was also a wonderful mentor with a strong personality. While my relationship with Jack lasted for three decades; he was a key mentor for a particular part of my early stage in life.

I also had a marathon coach, Keith Ollerenshaw, who also stood by me through thick and thin. He never intruded in my life but was always there when I needed him. He became a wonderful friend, and we were close up until he passed away. I will be forever indebted for his friendship and mentorship which has stood me in good stead.

When I moved overseas I connected with a business leader, Guy Dennider, who I had worked for in Belgium and who led a full and diverse life. He was someone who thought I was placed with him so he could guide me and direct me to the next stage in life, which he did over a number of years. I recall that he was blunt with his communication and had sized me up to a tee. His approach worked, and I can still remember to this day our discussions. He really opened a number of doors in my mind and was pivotal in me reassessing my approach to life. Again, I will be forever grateful.

Mentors come in various shapes and sizes and from many different parts of your life. Your mentors might be an uncle or aunt, teacher, sports coach, community group leader, church leader, your boss at your part-time job, grandparent, a trusted friend. Different people will have different skill sets, knowledge and experiences.

It's important when choosing a mentor to be clear that it's a commitment for both of you, and the mentoring relationship should have a defined structure to it that you're both happy with and a clear timeframe for review, perhaps once a year. As you grow and learn your needs change; similarly your mentor may have shifting priorities as well. It's best to have open and clear communication about the mentoring arrangement up front.

And don't be afraid to ask someone. Most people welcome the opportunity to help and mentor younger people, but they don't ask as they don't want to appear intrusive or pushy, especially if they're related to you. And if the person you ask is not able to do it, chances are they might know someone who can.

Parents can be mentors. Mine were more guiding lights. They helped me set my standards and values and caused me to set goals and ambitions, sometimes in a way that meant expectations were too great – this can cause you to see failure, not success.

IT'S NOT TOO EARLY

While it may seem too early to set yourself some clear goals about what you want to do and achieve, it's not. In the world of the 2020s and beyond there are few straight career paths, work will be more project-based and gig-orientated. So it's relevant to start looking at your goals and experiences with this firmly in mind, knowing that you need to revisit these at least once a year. And this is where having mentors comes in as well, as they can help you work through the ideas and options you have, which ones you want to prioritise and can manage, and how they will mesh together for you.

Again I reference Tom Peter's 1997 article as it's absolutely relevant to young people:

> *Reinvent yourself on a semi-regular basis. Start by writing your own mission statement, to guide you as CEO of Me Inc. What turns you on? Learning something new? Gaining recognition for your skills as a technical wizard? Shepherding new ideas from concept to market? What's your personal definition of success? Money? Power? Fame? Or doing what you love? However you answer these questions, search relentlessly for job or project opportunities that fit your mission statement. And review that mission statement every six months to make sure you still believe what you wrote.*

A good way of 'checking' your brand is by discovering the answer to these three questions. When people hear your name:

- What do they think about?
- What words would they associate your personal brand with?
- How would people describe you?

Then ask yourself these two questions:

- Have you *always* done what you said you would do? Have you fulfilled your promises on a *consistent* basis?
- What are your strengths and weaknesses, and what are you prepared to do to improve the weaknesses?

7 Early adulthood (early career: 20s to 30s)

By the time you are in your 20s you have the basis of conscious relevance management. You are moving from a space of being passive about who you are (and how you are perceived) to being more active in exploring just what it is you stand for, what your values are, what you want to achieve from life, and how you want to make a difference and make an impact. Of course everyone has to work through these and other personal goals, thoughts, behaviours and outcomes for themselves. But certainly in your 20s you are starting to think longer term about your mindset and behaviours.

And it's still a work in progress. Society – your family, friends, workplace and other groups – will give you *some* latitude if what you say doesn't match up with what you do, if you're inconsistent, unreliable, lazy or even worse. But this latitude does not last for long, and it can disappear overnight if you are involved in serious and perhaps unethical or illegal activities.

I hear you already asking, what about some sportspeople who seem to be given extraordinary amounts of latitude for bad or even illegal behaviour? This is an interesting one. I think there is a different 'degree of latitude' shown towards high achievers in sports and in business and other fields. The great success of the sports star or businessperson at some level transcends what would otherwise be regarded as unacceptable, although in most cases there is a decline in their reputation, earnings and therefore relevance as a result. Take Tiger Woods as one example. He's on the comeback trail, but he's nowhere near as dominant a golfer as he was, and does not command the same sponsorship nor reverence as he did. Andre Agassi was able to craft a positive future after a tennis career that went off the rails, as did John McEnroe. It remains to be seen if Nick Kyrgios can, or even wants to.

And then we have examples in business such as Alan Bond, John Elliott, Clive Palmer, Donald Trump, Michael Milken, Steve Vizard and Dick Pratt. There'll always be exceptions, and there seems to be more at the highest levels of sports and business, but they are largely exceptions.

For most of us though, our 20s is the time to build the foundations for our future, and it's a journey not a destination, particularly if you want to have and maintain relevance over the various stages of your life.

BUILDING RELEVANCE

In your early 20s, your relevance across family, friends, business and the wider community is in significant flux. While different for everyone and there'll always be exceptions, for most people their relevance and impact might look something like this:

- **Direct family:** Less relevance as you move out of home and head out on your own.
- **Friends:** More relevance as this becomes the group you spend most of your time with, and there may be partners in this group as well.
- **Business:** Whether you're employed, starting your own business or working as a gig worker, your business network and community takes on increasing relevance, and your friend and colleague groups will often cross over. Relevance with decision makers and leaders in your business or sector is important, and the key to developing your relevance to them is visibility.
- **Community:** Depending on your commitment to groups and organisations outside your work (sport and recreation, religious, arts and culture, environment, health, community-based groups and so on), your relevance to these may be increasing as you take on leadership roles. Taking on leadership roles in these areas may also help you with relevance and visibility in your business sphere.

As we've noted above, at this stage of life you are probably developing an interconnection between some of the key areas where you are relevant, and there's probably a melding of your work and social life and you're starting to realise the importance of networking and connections between the different spheres.

You've no doubt heard the phrase 'it's not what you know, it's who you know', and whether you like it or not that's how business and society work. I've often heard young people say they don't want their parents to use their networks to get them a job, that they can do it on their own, and many do. However, what most parents and other adults are actually offering is something much more nuanced. What they are offering is to 'open the door' to a job or role. It's then how you behave, perform and present yourself that will determine whether you are offered the job, and then if you keep it. This goes for internships as well.

And if the person offering to assist you is not your parent, the adult is effectively putting their reputation on the line by offering to help, as they're saying to the company, 'I'd like you to consider this person as I think they would be suitable for the role and I support them.'

BUILDING CREDIBILITY

It's hard to have a high level of credibility and relevance in your early to mid 20s as you're just starting out. Quite frankly, you don't know that much as you simply haven't had enough time to gain experience. That said, if you've taken active roles in community and other organisations in your mid to late teens, you might have developed a set of leadership skills, communication skills, capabilities and connections that others have not.

In Australian culture there's a reticence to engage in personal branding; it's seen by some as 'showy', egotistical, self-promotion. A better way to look at it as ensuring that the people you want to be relevant to now and in the near future need to know you exist and they're not going to seek you out – you have to find ways to be visible and credible to them.

Overlaid on this is the changing nature of the workforce at all levels. Even those coming out of university need to do everything they can to stand out from their peers to secure a position in a professional services firm, a start-up, a scale-up or other type of company. Job insecurity is no longer confined to low-skilled workers; highly skilled professions – including law, computer programming and finance – are all moving towards the gig paradigm. David Weil from the Heller School for Social Policy at Brandeis University in Boston and visiting professor at University of Sydney Business School recently noted that job insecurity is working its way up the skill ladder. In the US, contract lawyers are commonplace, and half of Google's employees are contract workers, including programmers. Weil notes that:

> *This idea that if you go to school or get a skill and you will be protected – that is not the case any more.*[1]

The competition is fierce, so you have to understand that you need to build a personal brand early so you're more visible and seen as more relevant to specific employers. You need to work out your speciality and uniqueness and go for it. It may well change in the future, but in your 20s you need to be aware of the fact that you can and should differentiate yourself and actively work on brand you. The sooner you start the more adept you'll be at pulling together the perhaps disparate parts of yourself through self-reflection, self-evaluation, realisation, action and delivery.

BUILDING VISIBILITY

A lot of young professionals complain that they get no respect even though they often have an advanced education and a rich portfolio

1 https://www.smh.com.au/business/workplace/wage-theft-now-a-problem-for-high-skilled-workers-20190816-p52hrd.html

of work, volunteer and internship experience. The only problem? They're not visible to senior leaders. No one can 'see' you because you're not at the executive tables, especially if you're the assistant or intern (although hot-desking and agile offices mean that in many companies you could well be sitting next to the CEO or other senior leaders).

There's a solution for this. Social media means thousands of people can 'see' you and follow your work and leadership. Social media can make you more visible to all the right people – if you use it well, and if you market yourself with professionalism and authenticity.

The reality is that in your 20s you *have* to be online and using social media in a way that tells people who you are and invites them to connect with you. And what better way to do that than with your personal brand.

You may think social media is not for you, and depending on what you regard as social media and how you use it, this could well be the case. Social media to a large degree has become commoditised as people have used it irresponsibly to build their personal brand. However, if used correctly with the right focus, intention and clear objectives, you can build a strong and highly visible profile.

Your personal brand should represent the value you are able to consistently deliver to those you are serving, both inside and outside the workplace – it's not an ongoing summary of what you've done, who you've worked with and your successes. By all means share these occasionally. But focus on the outcomes you've worked with others to achieve, or supported others in, and provide some insights or commentary on relevant topics in your area of work. The latter could even give you a great reason to call up and seek an interview with some industry leaders in your area of interest. You'd be surprised how open they might be to speaking with younger people with some drive and passion.

Critically, be consistent at engaging. Most platforms and search engines like regular engagement across different mediums and through text, video and audio.

As Glenn Llopis writes:

> *View your personal brand as a trademark; an asset that you must protect while continuously moulding and shaping it. Your personal brand is an asset that must be managed with the intention of helping others benefit from having a relationship with you and/or by being associated with your work and the industry you serve.*[2]

Another approach to increasing your visibility is to market yourself while you're training or at university through applying for internships, part-time jobs and volunteer roles. Applying for jobs and roles will force you to get specific about your core traits and unique skill set – in short, to differentiate yourself. No one else is going to do this for you.

And if you're looking to join the ranks of business or a professional firm, you need to get your act together on LinkedIn, and work out what other specific industry platforms are out there and get on them with the right profile (both visual and words). There's plenty of advice and insights available in books and online if you're not sure how or where to start.[3]

---

2 https://www.forbes.com/sites/glennllopis/2013/04/08/personal-branding-is-a-leadership-requirement-not-a-self-promotion-campaign/#55a5413b226f

3 A good resource is Dan Schawbel, who has written a couple of books on personal branding and career success (including *Me 2.0: Build a powerful brand to achieve career success*) as well as several articles in *Personal Branding* magazine.

One tip Dan shares is: *'Protect and promote your brand as much as possible.* Protecting your personal brand is extremely important because there are other people in the world with your name and if you fail to register your name on social networks and your domain name, someone else will. Also, you'll want to command your Google results because employers will be searching for you.'[4]

So when was the last time you did a Google search on your name? What did it come up with? What do you need to do to change what comes up ... what people see when they research you?

HOW MENTORING CAN HELP GROW YOUR RELEVANCE AND DISTIL YOUR VALUES

Firstly, you need to have the foresight and humility to ask to be mentored. This means you need to have a level of self-awareness, you need to have reflected on your strengths and weaknesses, and taken a reality check of why you are where you are, what you might need to change, or at least the areas you need some help with. This sounds easy, but many people don't ever do this, let alone in their 20s.

Secondly, you need to give serious thought to who you would like to be mentored by, and why. If you're not clear on this, a mentor will not simply 'pop up' and offer. Similarly, if you're not clear about the areas you want to develop, explore or work on, or able to articulate these to your potential mentor and what level of commitment you are prepared to put into this relationship, it's less likely someone will value mentoring you.

I've had mentors throughout my life, initially without consciously knowing that's what I was doing, and then by age 18 I made

4 https://www.fastcompany.com/1260055/personal-branding-young-professionals-interview-dan-schawbel-author-me-20

a conscious decision to seek out a mentor to help me achieve my personal sporting goal of being a cross-country and long-distance runner.

As I have moved through life I have gravitated to those people who have wisdom and understanding of areas of particular interest to me, such as business, leadership and the dynamics of international business. I found several mentors who guided and supported me, and I'm grateful for their interest in me. When I wanted help to identify a niche in the market for our business and seek expertise, I sought advice on who could be there to advise me. Some of these people were advisers and consultants, others were giving me their time.

I've now finished my executive career and I continue to have advisers and mentors. I never stop learning and benefiting from my mentors' and other professionals' experiences and expertise. I feel privileged that my mentors are prepared to take an interest in my wellbeing and career. I'm always interested in learning and growing, and part of this for me now is mentoring others as I've been mentored.

I now mentor younger people who have an ambition like I did and seek guidance and advice. I do this with great pleasure and enthusiasm as it's a joy to see them grow, develop, succeed and realise their ambitions and true potential.

Mentors are different from coaches. A mentoring relationship is usually more formal than a coach and is focused more on your journey than a specific outcome, on your thinking, self-awareness and insight rather than execution and delivery.

Jo Burston, serial entrepreneur and mentor to 12 people and someone who has had three mentors, provides a good description about the difference between a coach and mentor:

> *A business coach is someone who is strictly working on the fundamental processes of your business that may or may not have the experience you're seeking in the journey you're trying to go on. But a mentor looks at you as a whole person and whole entrepreneur.*
>
> *It's not just how you work in your business life but it's about who you are, what your drivers are, what your purpose is, how you take care of yourself as well as how you retain a network of support whether it's family, friends or other business people.*[5]

In your 20s is a good time to consider finding a mentor. They could be someone in your workplace at a more senior level, someone from your industry or outside it, or someone in a leadership position in your sporting or community group.

In terms of developing your relevance, visibility and impact, a mentor can help you accelerate your career and the future impact you want to have if you work with them the right way. Depending on where you are in your 20s, a mentor can:

- help you find your track or career starting point
- get you back on track if you've diverted
- help you focus on the future and options available, and what options to consider

---

5 https://www.businessinsider.com.au/7-simple-strategies-to-finding-an-excellent-mentor-2015-8

- guide you through a clear assessment of your values, behaviours and perceptible reality (what others know you for and as), and work through if and how to change
- open doors and provide connections
- act as a sounding board for major decisions, challenging situations and ethical dilemmas.

Mentoring is a two-way street that requires a commitment from both parties, and as you're just starting out on this journey this means significant effort by you. You have to work harder and longer than those around you and deliver value to your mentor if you're in a workplace mentoring environment.

Here's some feedback from people in their 20s who have been mentored:

> *'Professional mentors have the same impact on young professionals as to what Boy Scout leaders and rugby coaches have on a child. They offer overwhelming support and motivation to help mould young professionals into who they will become, and in a tough job market, they're prepared to keep them positive and motivated through job searches, interviews, rejections, and successes.'*

> *'Mentors have usually encountered the same experiences young professionals will soon face. They have firsthand stories on how they overcame obstacles, or how they failed. Because of these experiences, they can help new professionals determine what steps to take in their career, and can offer support when it is time to make a big step in a new direction.'*

'Mentors see beyond the everyday lazy young person, recognise the hard workers, and share the lessons they've learned to better prepare young professionals in their careers.'[6]

'I firmly believe that mentorship is the best path to career success, hands down. The benefits that you can gain from a good mentor relationship can outweigh grad school, natural ability, and even dumb luck.'[7]

SELF-REFLECTION AND AWARENESS

A critical component of developing a strong sense of self, of your values, behaviours and actions is the capability for self-reflection. Here are some questions you might ask yourself and others around you:

- What are your strengths and weaknesses?
- How would people describe you?
- Are you honest and reliable?
- Your private persona or character must be congruent with your public brand. Are you the same person on the inside as you are on the outside?
- What are your intentions? Are your actions for the greater good and valued ideals?
- What are your personal brand values?
- Is your personal brand a positive brand that people would look up to and admire?

---

6 https://www.huffpost.com/entry/why-young-professionals-n_b_1842738

7 https://www.forbes.com/sites/chrismyers/2016/02/21/mentorship-is-key-to-career-success-for-young-professionals/#2581f95221b8

- Where and how would people validate your personal brand reputation?
- Historically, have you *always* done what you said you would do? Have you fulfilled your promises on a *consistent* basis?
- When people hear your name, what do they think about? What words would they associate your personal brand with?[8]

When you receive feedback that's not positive or does not match your own view of yourself, do you care enough to change? You are the only one who can undertake this.

As I said earlier, everyone has a personal brand, whether you like it or not. The fact is that when people think of you, they have some kind of impression in their minds about who you are and what you stand for.

The real question is, is your personal brand a good one or not?

What do people in your professional circle think of you? Do people even know who you are?

Your 20s is the time to ask yourself these and other hard questions and then act on the responses.

8 https://www.linkedin.com/pulse/8-laws-personal-branding-brian-tracy-paraphrasing-sheriff-osni/

8 **Professional maturity** (prime career: 30s to mid 50s)

By your early to mid 30s you are progressing in your chosen field or profession and should have established a position within your industry, company or firm. You also may have moved roles within a company or into a new opportunity. It's also becoming more and more likely that as your industry or profession changes to meet the continuing pressures of business in a low-growth, uncertain economic environment, parts of your role will be changing and you might be out of a job *or* the nature of how you work will have changed or will soon.

Welcome to the world of *volatility*, *uncertainty*, *complexity* and *ambiguity* (VUCA). In this world there is no job for life, and it's more than likely the career pathways that used to be a given in whatever sector or profession you are in changed a while back. This is why you need to actively manage your personal brand, reputation and relevance.

With corporate and business disruption occurring faster than ever, your only real currency is your intellectual property connected with your reputation, as opposed to what you create and for what company.

In your 30s it's time to take stock of just where you are in terms of your relevance and impact. If you've actively managed 'brand you' up to this point you should have built a solid foundation, but your relevance and impact are not a 'set and forget' exercise. Now is the time for you to review your values, behaviours and networks to build on and consolidate your relevance, and therefore make a greater impact in the areas you choose to focus on. This means, among other things, filling in some of the gaps that you didn't know you had when you were younger, and this requires a large dose of self-awareness. For many this is hard when they perceive themselves to be close to the top of their game, hitting their goals, and relevant to their core groups. But beware, this is where your ego can outstrip your capability.

It's also a challenging time in terms of juggling your relevance across the different spheres … the time when you're probably more relevant across all aspects of your life: family, work, and community. In your 30s and 40s you're more than likely to be partnered, become a parent, and be in or close to a leadership role in your chosen field and possibly the wider community. Each of these roles requires you to deeply understand your key purpose and values in life, as they will drive where you spend your time and how you make an impact in each of these.

This said, there are always exceptions, as the following list shows. All these achievers have high recognition and relevance in their areas and all are at the younger end of the 30 to 50s band:

- Dr Rebecca Johnson, Wildlife Forensic Scientist, conservation geneticist and Chief Scientist of the Australian Museum

- Eddie Woo, a mathematics teachers and winner of the 2018 Australia's Local Hero Award
- Bri Lee, author and founder of Hot Chicks with Big Brains
- Dr Belinda Liddell, the mental health researcher recognised as one of the Top 5 young scientists in the ABC awards in 2018
- Dr Dominique Tanner, geologist at the University of Wollongong studying how precious metals are created in undersea volcanoes.[1]

YOU ARE NOT YOUR WORK

After 40-plus years in business and working across a range of community organisations, I've come to understand that most people think about their reputation and relevance in relation to *what they do* (their job) as opposed to *who they are*. As a result, many people in their 30s and 40s burn out as their life is framed by their job as they focus intensely on being known (relevant) for what they do. Many become caught up in the status trap of wanting to earn more to achieve or obtain a lifestyle commensurate with their peer group or their own views about status and society.

The real challenge with this approach is that it's simply not sustainable and is certainly not conducive to achieving relevance across the different aspects of your life. For you to develop and build a sustainable personal brand in your 30s, 40s and into your 50s you need to have a level of self-awareness and insight (emotional intelligence) to build your reputation and relevance across the different aspects of your life. You need to develop a different mindset to who you

1 https://www.abc.net.au/radio/programs/top5/science/

are, what you stand for, and how this will drive your contribution and impact.

You can't let your work frame the way people think about you – this creates a box that's hard to get out of.

BUILDING ON YOUR CORE VALUES

The period of your 30s and 40s is often a time when priorities are changing. Marriage, parenthood and increased responsibilities at work or in your business often prompt a reassessment of values and where you want to be relevant and make an impact. You may have thought about your values in the past but not done anything proactive about living them. It's a bit like all those company vision statements that we've all seen and read and then promptly forgotten.

Values without actions are nothing.

Leading sports performance coach Jonah Oliver talks about putting values into action, about setting goals in service of your values. He says that if you only have goals people are more than likely to reset if they feel they're not going to achieve them, whereas if the goals are connected to something that matters (your values) you'll keep striving in the service of something that matters.[2]

That's why this is the time to revisit and build on your core values and deeply interrogate what you are known for, what you want to be known for and the personal journey you need to undertake to bridge the gap between them. You need to understand who you are so you can clearly assess opportunities and risks along this journey.

---

2 https://jonaholiver.com/

TRUST IS ESSENTIAL

With a lot of demand on your time at this stage of your life and career, it's important that you move away from the old business management model of power and control as it's not sustainable *and* possibly not aligned to your values. It's also important to understand your relevance to your family, communities and society, as this is what gives us all meaning.

Like a consumer brand, the key element of your personal brand is trust. Trust is the foundation of all relationships, business and personal. If you want to build relevance in your 30s and 40s you have to build trust and networks of trusted relationships.

As Jeremy Durant from Bop Design noted in his blog post 15 Crazy Branding Stats You Need to Know, over 60% of customers have a relationship with a brand because they share the same values in their life.[3] I believe the percentage would be much higher for personal brands.

There are many brands that consumers are passionate about and totally committed to and therefore they have become iconic and stood the test of time. Tabasco is a brand that is adored by its users. Apple consumers love the brand and swear by it, although there's also a large consumer cohort who dislike Apple and swear by PCs and other phone or computer brands. Moët has been the standard for champagnes ever since Claude Moët established Moët et Cie in 1743.

Professional relationships are built on trust and commitment. We can all have a strategic plan, a clear vision and strong communication skills, however if your boss, colleagues or team do not trust in

---

3 https://www.bopdesign.com/bop-blog/2015/10/15-crazy-branding-stats/

you and each other, the desired results will not follow and you won't make the impact you want.

According to Paul Zak, founding director of the Centre for Neuroeconomic Studies at Claremont Graduate University in California, the statistics around their research into trust are startling:

> *Compared with people at low-trust companies, people at high-trust companies report: 74% less stress, 106% more energy at work, 50% higher productivity, 13% fewer sick days, 76% more engagement, 29% more satisfaction with their lives and 40% less burnout.*[4]

On the one hand, if you are not someone who is trustworthy (either in part or in full) you won't have the relevance or impact you desire or strive for as a leader or as part of a team. You'll need to deeply self-reflect about your values and your behaviours and decide if you want to change and then take action. On the other hand, if you're working in a low-trust company, is this really where you want to be as it does not reflect your values, you can't act in alignment with your values and you won't be as effective and relevant as you want to be.

If you are moving into leadership roles in your organisation it's mission critical that you undertake an honest self-assessment of where you are at with your values, behaviours and the perceptible reality in your spheres (refer to the model we shared on page 61).

Given the importance of trust in our values and behaviour, how can you improve the culture of trust in your team, group, organisations, family?

---

4 https://hbr.org/2017/01/the-neuroscience-of-trust

I've shared the matrix developed by Jon Spinney[5] below as it links closely with our discussions about your values and the values I've shared in chapter 2). Review this and tick the boxes you believe are attributes you exhibit consistently. And review Jon's thoughts on trust:

> *Trust is a firm belief in the reliability, truth, ability, or strength of someone. Trust is earned. It's built over time. Trust is a choice – a verb – something one DOES.*

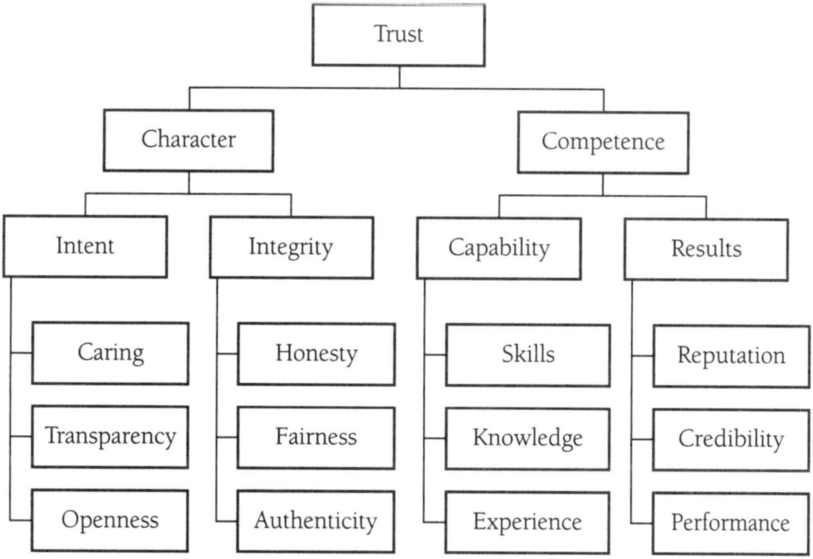

WHERE ARE YOU SPENDING YOUR TIME?

As we've noted previously, at this stage in your life you have various commitments across the key areas of your life and it's important

---

5 http://jonspinney.com/thoughts/2016/6/21/building-trust?rq=trust. Used with permission.

that you make conscious decisions about the time you spend across these different groups and how you spend that time within each one of them. It's next to impossible to have maximum relevance across all four main groups (although some do try), so it's important to understand what's important to you and why, and what your real purpose is, as this will help you navigate the daily, monthly and yearly decisions you have to make about the options that are presented to you.

The decisions may be different for males and females. More women than men choose to take time out of the workforce to care for their young family. For some, their family is their primary focus of relevance (although by far not their only focus of relevance) for a period of time. Others choose to prioritise their family and work. Whatever family dynamic you are in at this stage, it will be one of two primary areas of relevance for the majority.

In terms of your work area, it's important in terms of managing your relevance to review where you are spending your time, with whom, and how if you want to grow your relevance. You also need to have clarity about how you are ensuring you are visible and what you are contributing to build your profile and relevance. While this may seem brash, too calculated, pushy, or self-orientated, it's none of these.

Developing and growing your personal brand and profile based on your values and actions is how you are going to be relevant and have an impact in the areas you care about. If you are clear about your purpose and values and take action to live these you will create a positive impact.

So, assess where you are spending your time networking. What level of engagement are you delivering and what are you receiving?

There's no point joining work groups and industry organisations and participating in charity and workplace events if you're not fully committed. What's the point if your engagement level is low? Your fulfilment level will be low as well … you won't be making an impact.

Where can you effectively network and who do you want to network with? These are critical questions to explore. If you're seeking to build a wider profile in your sector, you're going to have to seek out the best groups and organisations to engage with, and then engage consistently. This applies to your workplace as well. If you want to build your profile and relevance, you're going to have to put your hand up for new projects, work harder, smarter and longer, and build new connections across the company … be proactive.

WHO ARE YOU SPENDING YOUR TIME WITH?

One of the more challenging aspects of personal branding and relevance is exploring who you associate with and why. By the time you are in your early to mid career phase, you will have formed associations with a wide range of people for a variety of reasons. If you want to maximise the relevance and impact of 'brand you', you need to be able to stand back from simply engaging those you've come across and formed relationships with and assess if they are relationships that are aligned to your values and where you can make an impact.

The most obvious starting point is reviewing where you are working (if you are working for a company, organisation or firm rather than for yourself – the latter might be a hard one to assess, although not impossible as you *could* sack yourself; that's now called reinvention).

The company you are working for

It's important to assess the company you are working for. Does it share your values? What is its purpose? Does this align with your values and purpose? If not, what are you going to do about this? As your values and actions will not be aligned, others will 'see' this and your relevance and impact will be less than it can be.

As the saying goes:

> *You can fool all the people some of the time, and some of the people all the time, but you cannot fool all the people all the time.*

Most importantly, you can try to fool yourself but that invariably doesn't work, as stress levels, health and relationships suffer if you're trying to be someone you're not. Quite apart from that, why would you spend a large part of your life working for a company that doesn't share your values and purpose? For example, if you are a strong advocate for physical health and wellness, would you work for a tobacco, fast food or soft drink company knowing the rising rates of obesity and the long-term health impacts of these products? Thousands of people do … but would you?

Similarly, if you are passionate about climate change and its impact on the planet, would you work for a coal company or oil company? Again, thousands of people do, but they are not you. How would you feel if you did, and the company you worked for was responsible for one of the worst human-caused disasters in the world, like the Exxon Valdez spill in Prince William Sound in Alaska in 1989, or the Deepwater Horizon oil spill in 2010?

Or, how would you feel working for a bank in Australia during and after the Royal Commission, or 2GB or the Macquarie Media network, a gambling company, or Origin Energy or Eraring Power Station, the latter of which came under intense criticism for exceeding already generous pollution limits.[6]

Those associated with companies such as Blue Sky Private Equity, Quintis, Queensland Nickel and others will clearly be assessing the impact on their reputations (and relevance) as a result of the non-performance, administration or liquidation of these businesses. Of course, the fallout from the 1987 stock market crash ended the high-flying careers of many a senior-level businessperson, although some from the 2008 GFC seem to have navigated a way through the corporate reputational jungle.

We all need to work, and we all have a choice of who we work with and for. The point is that you need to truly test whether who you are working with and for share your values, and if they don't, what – if anything – are you going to do about it?

These are uncomfortable questions to ask yourself, but they need to be explored if you are going to live by your values, be a trusted and respected person in and across your communities, and have relevance and impact.

The company you keep

Separate to the organisations you work with and for (although they are sometimes connected) are the people you associate with. Again, this is a challenging discussion to have with yourself as it crosses so many unspoken beliefs, values and societal norms. This is particularly so in my view in Australia, where we have a range of cultural norms attached to mateship, that catchall word that covers everyone

---

6 https://coastcommunitynews.com.au/central-coast/news/2017/09/environmental-report-slams-vales-point-eraring-power-stations/, https://www.envirojustice.org.au/powerstations/

from someone we've only just met to a long-standing friend, and embodies equality, loyalty and friendship.

The reality is that guilt by association is alive and well because it's an emotional response. Think about the Australian banks. Clearly, not everyone who works at a bank is responsible for the over-charging, fee-for-no-service or non-payment of claims uncovered in the Royal Commission, but there's an element of guilt by association.

Or what about those who worked with Bernie Madoff, the former investment adviser and financier who is currently residing in a US federal prison after his Ponzi scheme was uncovered? And then there's Harvey Weinstein, once one of the most powerful men in Hollywood, or Sepp Blatter, the former head of FIFA.

Closer to home, those associated with CPA Australia and Alex Malley have been impacted following the revelations about the allocation of CPA Australia's funds to promote Malley rather than CPA Australia, among other suspect directors' payments and poor project decisions. Many of CPA's board members resigned, and the status of the organisation itself has suffered greatly as a result.

Interestingly, as noted previously, the wider community seems to have a much higher degree of tolerance for unacceptable or illegal behaviour from sportspeople provided their performance on the field continues.

Donating your time and knowledge

Being considered about who you work with and for extends to your activities outside your workplace and through to your community activities. Engaging in not-for-profit work is a valuable and rewarding thing to do, and I've spent most of my adult life on committees, boards and foundations donating my services and knowledge.

Involvement in the not-for-profit sector is an excellent way for someone in their 30s and 40s to extend their network and create meaningful new professional relationships outside the confines of your specific area. However, it's critical that, as with the organisation you work for and people you work with, you ensure that the NFP you are joining and the board or committee members share the same values as you do. If not, find one that does.

NFPs are not immune from illegal or less than charitable practices, so you need to undertake significant due diligence of the board members and senior executives before agreeing to join. One only needs to be reminded of the demise of the Shane Warne Foundation in 2016,[7] the Immigrant Women's Health Service in 2017 and Save A Horse Australia to see the impact of being connected to a charity whose governance is less than best practice. You should ask to see their policies around governance, conflicts of interest, related-party transactions, the administration costs ratio, and the tenure of board members and executives. If you're not sure what you should be looking for, this is where your mentor can provide invaluable advice and insight.

Mentors

What personal development are you undertaking? If you don't have a mentor, go and find one – they'll be one of the best investments you can make. Many organisations provide a mentoring program. Seek it out. Find out what you need to do to be selected and take action. If your organisation doesn't have such a program, find a mentor through your industry organisations or ask colleagues, your boss

---

7 https://www.smh.com.au/business/the-real-story-of-how-the-shane-warne-foundation-fell-apart-20160211-gmrbjs.html, https://www.smh.com.au/national/shane-warne-shuts-charity-to-avoid-potential-deregistration-20170111-gtpn7z.html

or an industry leader, and act on their recommendations. And, if need be, pay for it.

If you have a mentor, make sure you are revisiting your goals and progressing towards them. Have you grown (stretched your mind, body and soul) over the past year, or have you fallen off the pace? Do you need to recommit time to personal development and growth? Unless you are growing, you're going backwards, so it's up to you to proactively ensure you are keeping up with your skills, industry trends and changes.

Your mentor can and will also help you assess how 'brand you' is going. They will provide you with direct and honest feedback on your performance, growth and value. It's up to you to decide what you do with this feedback and to talk through the steps you need to take with your mentor.

Your mentor is also the person who can deploy their network to help you build your own. Remember what we covered in the previous chapter: most people (especially your mentor) want to help you, but you have to ask. And all they can do is open the door; you have to be ready and prepared for when you walk through it.

YOUR BRAND BY DESIGN

Tom Peters way back in 1997 talked about how you market brand you, and his insights are still relevant today for those in their 30s to early 50s, so I've summarised them here:

- Try teaching a class at a community college, at your alma mater, within your industry association, even within your company. You'll build up confidence and recognition as an expert and increase your standing as a professional.

- If you're a better writer than you are a teacher, try contributing a column or opinion piece to your organisation's in-house newsletter or industry association newsletter or magazine. Try writing regular articles for LinkedIn (about 1000 words) and share these through your connections. Also read and comment on what other leaders and influencers are writing and sharing.
- If you're a better talker than you are a teacher or writer, try to get yourself on a panel discussion at a conference or sign up to make a presentation at a workshop. And you have the option of recording some short videos of your own and posting these on your page on LinkedIn or in a Group page. Or identify who the influencers are in your area and who has a podcast. Follow it, comment and engage, and then approach the person with an idea for a guest podcast.

Remember, everything you do, and choose not to do, communicates the value and character of brand you. Everything from the way you handle phone conversations to the email messages you send to the way you conduct business in a meeting is part of the larger message you're sending about your brand.

Partly it's a matter of substance: what you have to say and how well you say it. But it's also a matter of style. Do your online communications demonstrate a command of the technology? In meetings, do you keep your contributions short and to the point? Do you come across as assured and knowledgeable?

'INFLUENCE POWER'

Peters also discusses the important matter of 'influence power'. Our interpretation of this is relevance, but the message is the same, and in your 30s and 40s you should be fully engaged in all aspects of this.

Influence power is being known for making a significant contribution in your particular area. It's reputational power. If you are a consultant, you'd measure it by the number of CEOs who have your direct email address. If you are a scholar, you'd measure it by the number of times your publications are cited by other people. If you're an executive in a company you'd measure it by the number of special projects you're asked to lead, the leadership development programs you're selected for, the team leadership roles you're appointed to.

Getting and using power – intelligently, responsibly, and yes, powerfully – are essential skills for growing your brand. One of the things that attracts us to certain brands is the power they project. As a consumer, you want to associate with brands whose powerful presence creates a halo effect that rubs off on you, anything from the super brands like Louis Vuitton, Gucci, Bulgari and Rolex through to challenger brands such as Vans, Abercrombie & Fitch, Snapchat, Red Bull and Hollister, as well as some perennials like Ralph Lauren, Levi's, Lee and Nike.

To quote Peters directly:

> *Most important, remember that power is largely a matter of perception. If you want people to see you as a powerful brand, act like a credible leader. When you're thinking like brand You, you don't need org-chart authority to be a leader. The fact is you are a leader. You're leading You!*[8]

---

8 https://www.fastcompany.com/28905/brand-called-you?page=0,0

MAINTAINING RELEVANCE IN THE VUCA WORLD

It's important to understand that relevance is a dynamic journey and that the period of relevance in the executive and leadership world of organisations and firms is diminishing rapidly. CEO tenure in the US dropped from six to five years between 2013 and 2018.[9] The average tenure for a CEO is now five years and eight months for the ASX 200, and five years and two months for the FTSE 100 CEOs. Just 12% of ASX 200 CEOs and 11% of the FTSE 100 CEOs have served in their organisation for more than 10 years.[10] Executive roles would not be dissimilar. Combined with a change in how companies are organised – moving from top-down hierarchies to more agile and fast-moving, project-based work – it's critical for you to understand the short and longer term trend in the sector you're working in so you can adjust what your knowledge and skills are, how you project them ... how you stay relevant.

---

9 https://corpgov.law.harvard.edu/2018/02/12/ceo-tenure-rates/#targetText=In%20the%20past%20five%20years,at%20the%20end%20of%202017.

10 https://www.afr.com/work-and-careers/management/hayne-sparks-20-top-ceo-turnover-20181015-h16nar

9 Wisdom and retirement (late career: mid 50s onwards)

Given that I'm in this age bracket, this part of *Brand New Brand You* is close to my heart (figuratively and physically), and it's partly the transition that I've undertaken at this stage of my life that prompted me to write this book.

After 41 years as the CEO of our private family business, it was time for me to transition to the next phase of my life, so I resigned and took up the role as Chairman. I had no intention of holding on to the executive role as I was clear I wanted to create a different level of relevance outside the business, in other companies and in the community.

> *'Age is an issue of mind over matter. If you don't mind, it doesn't matter.'* – Mark Twain

Many senior executives, partners and managers don't have the option of determining when they'll move on to the next phase of their life; that's often decided by the policies of the organisation, restructuring, mergers, acquisitions, transformations or, in some case, administration and liquidation.

The terminology used to describe people over 50 is off-putting – for those of us over 50, that is. 'Older workers', 'mature-aged workers' and 'seniors'. Then there's the stereotypes of older workers: that they are resistant to change, out of date with current technologies, stuck in the hierarchical, top-down management models, don't or can't work hard and might need greater time off due to ill-health. At worst, older workers can be seen as overqualified, not as tech-savvy as younger professionals and more expensive than their younger counterparts. Some younger people even resent older people for crowding them out of roles and positions, for 'hanging around too long'.

The reality is if you're not healthy, tech savvy, keeping up your professional or other qualifications and interested and truly engaged with a wide variety of people, the benefits you can bring to a role will be outweighed by the fact that you haven't kept up.

YOUR RELEVANCE IS CHANGING AGAIN

At your mid-50s onwards your relevance across all spheres of your life is changing again.

You're past the 'fake it till you make it' stage (possibly a long time ago). At this stage you have to be real, engaged and generous with your insights and knowledge yet really open to new and different ways of working and leading ... and perhaps not leading.

You also have to change your mindset and become less 'boss' and instructional, more collaborative and engaged. This applies to your family and friends as well as in the workforce and community groups you're involved with. It's not about age, it's about your attitude; in fact, you don't want to be 'acting your age' as you need to change to maintain your relevance.

In your later 50s onwards, the gap between you and younger generations becomes larger and therefore the bridge between you and them longer. To maintain relevance you must change your methods of approaching business, the way you communicate with others, and how and where you express yourself.

> *'Your best thinking from three years ago is your biggest baggage today.'* – Dan Priestley

Unless you choose to be actively involved in the conversations across the different aspects of your life, you will be sidelined. As a result, you won't keep pace with the content and news around specific industry or macro trends or the discussions that are driving specific issues. For example, are you aware of the Statement of the Purpose of a Corporation that was published by the US Business Roundtable in August 2019 and the ensuing discussion about it?[1] If not, you're out of touch.

Alan Schwartz, the managing director of Trawalla Capital and the founder of the Universal Commons Project, is highly engaged about the debate about the purpose of business. In 2017, he commented that, 'I attribute many of the problems in our economy to the fact that profit and value are not aligned, so that it is possible to make a profit while destroying the environment or social cohesion and equally it is possible to create value – for example, reducing carbon emission or homelessness – but make a loss.'[2]

---

1 https://www.businessroundtable.org/business-roundtable-redefines-the-purpose-of-a-corporation-to-promote-an-economy-that-serves-all-americans

2 Jemima Whyte, 'Stakeholder Primacy Misses the Point: Schwartz', *AFR*, 2 September 2019, page 3.

Are you up to date with the latest trends and regulations in your industry? Do you know what economic and technology changes are affecting your area?

Do you really understand the changing demographics of Australia, and how this will impact on the declining percentage of the workforce that will be required to cover the costs of our ageing population? Have you read the recent Grattan Institute report on this topic, 'Generation Gap: Ensuring a fair go for younger Australians', rather than just the headlines in the newspaper?[3]

And are you aware of the cultural differences that underpin the business practices of our major trading partners: China, the Middle East, India and EU countries? If not, how can you expect to understand scaling an online business or the transformation of existing 'traditional businesses' for digital growth?

What was acceptable 10 or 15 years ago is no longer acceptable. Where does your response to these and other issues sit with your values? What and who are you prepared to support or not, based on your values? Are you willing to consider re-evaluating your viewpoint based on new information, or not? Sitting on the fence and not engaging will diminish your relevance not only in the business and not-for-profits you are engaged with but across your community and family.

Alongside changing your mindset, you need good judgement, self-awareness and trusted advisers as you review your options and who or what you become associated with, as there's much more at stake. If you thought making decisions about what organisations and people you wanted to be associated with when you were younger was challenging, it's significantly more serious in your 50s onwards

---

3 https://grattan.edu.au/report/generation-gap/

as there's much more to lose, and guilt by association will impact more on you.

So, how is your relevance changing across the different parts of your life?

- **Family/friends:** Children are growing up and may, or may not, be moving out of home. You may have a second, younger family, and if you do your relevance to your first family and children will be quite different to your current family. Step-parenting brings in a whole other array of challenges around relevance.

  It's likely you also have elderly parents requiring more time, attention and care. If you have siblings your relevance to them is also changing. Usually there's someone who takes on the lead role within the family in terms of discussions and management of elderly parents. There may also be issues around care and support for siblings and their children.

  Then there's your network of friends. Some may have retired, others will still be working (by choice or need). Depending on where your priorities are you may become less or more relevant to certain friends. Some may be living off past achievements and not across contemporary business trends or challenges, others will be as active as they have ever been.

- **Career:** At this stage it's likely you are moving through the end phase of an executive role, partnership or senior manager position. Your relevance in the organisation will likely be determined more by the organisation than you. If you want to stay relevant for longer you'd better make sure you're leading major projects within your organisation, leading teams of younger talent and taking higher profile roles and positions within your industry.

With your career coming to a close, you now have a range of options to choose from depending on your own circumstance:

- secure another role as you need to keep working
- become an interim executive as you want to keep working in your chosen field but want flexibility about how and when you work
- take board positions on ASX-listed companies, private companies or industry associations
- retire.

- **Community:** This can include chair or leadership positions on not-for-profits, foundations and government boards (you may have already taken on some NFP board roles in your late 40s and 50s as part of your forward planning). Think about Peter Cosgrove's career. General Sir Peter Cosgrove was Governor General of Australia from 2014 to 2019. A graduate from Duntroon Military College, Peter served in Vietnam and had a distinguished military career. He came to public prominence as commander of the International Force for East Timor (INTERFET), before being appointed Chief of Army from 2000 to 2002, and then Chief of the Defence Force from 2002 to 2005.

  After retiring from the Army, he served as leader of a taskforce helping to rebuild communities in Queensland after Cyclone Larry in 2006. He also served on the board of Qantas between 2005 and 2014, was Chancellor of the Australian Catholic University between 2010 and 2014, was Honorary

Patron in Chief of the ACT Veterans rugby club and Rosies Youth Mission, as well as Patron to the Australian Volunteer Coast Guard Association in 2015.

Someone who has had a different but no less interesting career pathway and transition is Ita Buttrose, now the Chairperson of the ABC. Ita was founding editor of *Cleo* then editor of *Australian Women's Weekly*.

In 2011 she was elected President of Alzheimer's Australia until the end of June 2014. She is currently an ambassador for Dementia Australia, and between 2013 and 2018 she was a panellist on the morning program *Studio 10*.

Among her many other public service and charitable activities, Buttrose is a patron of Women of Vision, World Vision Australia, the University of the Third Age, the Juvenile Diabetes Foundation of Australia, Amarant, the National Menopause Foundation, the Sydney Women's Festival, Safety House and the National Institute of Secretaries and Administrators. She is also an ambassador of the Australian Women Chamber of Commerce and Industry (AWCCI) and sits on the AWCCI Advisory Board.[4]

- **Public life:** This may be a complete change or reinvention. For example, Malcolm Turnbull moved from a highly successful business career to become the Prime Minister of Australia between 2015 and 2018, and Clive Palmer created his own political party and has contested a number of elections.

In reviewing all your options, it is important to understand that the relevance you've built up prior to this point across these groups

---

4 https://en.wikipedia.org/wiki/Ita_Buttrose

will change, and how it changes is up to you and will impact those around you, your partner, family and friends. You've been on a pathway for 10 to 20 years (or more), now you are transitioning and this will impact on them.

Whatever option you choose, if you're moving on from an executive career or partnership role where you've been for a while, the support systems within that role will no longer be there. You're out on your own ... and this is where your relevance becomes one of your strongest, if not your strongest, attribute. It's a challenging time for many people as they find it hard to shift from seeing their work as the key part of their brand and identity to *who they are and what they do*. You are no longer Jo Bloggs from Rio Tinto, you're just Jo Bloggs. If you haven't worked on your relevance before now, you need to get moving lest you become irrelevant in some or all parts of your life.

WHAT DOES OVER 55 NOW LOOK LIKE?

If you want to keep working, or need to keep working, what does over 55 now look like?

It's vital to have new skill sets and an understanding of the mega trends – AI, data analytics and the internet of things (IoT) – and how these are transforming businesses – *all businesses*. You also need to understand the changing nature of business; it's no longer top-down and hierarchical but more project-based, fluid and agile. If this isn't your experience you need to get up to speed.

I've quoted Tom Peters earlier in the book, and I am about to again. Even though the following quote is directed at someone in their 20 or 30s, it also applies to someone in their 50s, plus it brings home the importance of a change of mindset … from linear management to projects.

> *One key to growing your power is to recognise the simple fact that we now live in a project world. A project-based world is ideal for growing your brand: projects exist around deliverables, they create measurables, and they leave you with braggables. If you're not spending at least 70% of your time working on projects, creating projects, or organising your (apparently mundane) tasks into projects, you are sadly living in the past. Today you have to think, breathe, act, and work in projects.*[5]

And Peters wrote this in 1997, before the term 'gig economy' had even been invented and before gig work started moving into the professional and executive suites (or hot desks).

WHAT'S THE FUTURE OF YOU?

It's over. No more vertical. No more ladder. That's not the way careers work anymore. Linearity is out. A career is now a checkerboard. Or even a maze. It's full of moves that go sideways, forward, slide on the diagonal, even go backwards when that makes sense. (It often does.) A career is a portfolio of projects that teach you new skills, gain you new expertise, develop new capabilities, grow your colleague set, and constantly reinvent you as a brand.

As you scope out the path your 'career' will take, remember:

> *The last thing you want to do is become a manager. Like 'résumé,' 'manager' is an obsolete term. It's practically synonymous with*

5 https://www.fastcompany.com/28905/brand-called-you?page=0,0

'dead-end job'. What you want is a steady diet of more interesting, more challenging, more provocative projects.[6]

In your 50s and onwards you absolutely need to understand the project-based nature of the future work that's available to you. And if you are not familiar with the terms 'gig economy' (for professionals), 'interim executive' or 'portfolio career' you're already trailing behind the biggest trend in the global workforce.

CHANGING HOW YOU WORK

At this stage in your life, unless you are actively engaged with the conversations happening in your industry and communities you'll become less and less relevant, and being active requires a different level of effort to be engaged and proactive. It also probably requires a different approach to how you currently operate. For some it's a home office, for others a permanent office in a CBD location with a dedicated or shared support person. For others it's working from a shared workspace, or being completely agile and working from anywhere.

Then there's the challenge of technology, both in terms of keeping across it from a functional perspective and understanding the mega trends that are occurring in the digital revolution we're now well in to. This requires significant effort given the constant and fast pace of change and its impact on traditional business models. I recommend reading Kevin Kelly's book *The Inevitable*[7] which discusses the 12 technological forces that will shape our future and will, by their very nature, impact on the future of business, work, recreation, community and interactions between and across cultures.

---

6 https://www.fastcompany.com/28905/brand-called-you?page=0,0

7 Kelly, Kevin. *The Inevitable: Understanding the 12 technological forces that will shape our future*, Viking, 2016.

THE INTERIM REVOLUTION

The speed at which change is disrupting business globally is rapid. Technology innovations now come so fast the biggest challenge for medium and large companies, firms and partnerships is that most lack the capability, speed and agility to respond to this rapid change. Not only has this meant that business transformations are upending the traditional 'safe' executive level of organisations, but that the capability and speed gap is widening. The response from companies is to flatten their executive and management structures while moving to using freelance, high-calibre professionals on short- or long-term assignments (gigs) to solve business problems and drive transformation programs or change projects. If you thought the gig economy was only for Uber drivers, food delivery, computer programmers, virtual assistants and other blue-collar workers, think again.

> *'The tension between organisations optimised for predictability and the unpredictable world they inhabit has reached a breaking point.'* – Responsive.org Manifesto

The interim executive (or portfolio career) option is significantly more advanced in the US, UK and Europe than Australia, which according to Watermark International Interim Executive lead Jacinta Whelan is about five to six years behind. Watermark International undertakes an annual survey of the Australian Interim marketplace, and in 2019 the survey noted that:

> *70% of assignments were for business transformation/change management and specialist skills not currently available in house and 48% were for other C-Suite roles. The main categories within business transformation were functional transformation, cultural*

change/transformation, turnaround, business resource, strategy, growth, acquisitions, change in operating model and restructuring. The soft skill sets most in demand were stakeholder engagement (37%), ability to quickly demonstrate capability (29%) and quickly understand internal policies to navigate successfully.[8]

This reinforces the Tom Peters observation that the 'manager' role is a dead end. As Jacinta Whelan comments:

Companies are looking for people who have the whole package and who have currency. Interim executives need to have current reference points for projects that they have worked on and need to show what role they played in their success. There's no point talking about a project you completed 15 years ago or even 5 years ago. You're only as good as your last project and you need to demonstrate this.[9]

If you want to remain relevant and use your knowledge and skills in a more hands-on way this is certainly a great option, but it does require a change of mindset, and from all accounts you need to park your ego, not be focused on the accoutrements of executive life when you're on assignment, and enjoy the challenges of project-based defined outcomes and timeframes.

THE BOARDROOM PATHWAY

Many senior executives move into the boardroom post their executive career. If this is something you're thinking of doing, it's important

---

8 Watermark International Interim Executive Annual Report, 2019.

9 Interview with Jacinta Whelan, 19 July 2019.

to actually start on this before you retire or are restructured out of your current role – as early as in your 40s. Taking on a not-for-profit board position is a great way to learn about the role of a board member, extend your networks, give back to the community and make an impact.

However, if you have not built up your networks or been active in your industry and community outside your executive role, it's going to be hard to be appointed to the boards you want. The traditional pathway for board roles is usually a not-for-profit board, unlisted company board, then public company board.

And you need to be careful about which boards you choose to join. Many a board director has suffered as a result of being on the board of a not-for-profit or listed company that has collapsed or been linked to illegal or corrupt practices. The board members of these companies suffered significant impact on their reputations and therefore relevance and impact. The most recent examples are of a number of board members and directors of our large banks and financial institutions: Ken Henry from NAB, Catherine Brenner from AMP and George Venardos from IOOF, as well as several board members and executives from other companies. Interestingly, by May 2019 significant board renewal at AMP meant that 70% of the directors in place at the beginning of 2018 had left or stepped down – no director remaining had served more than two-and-a-half years.[10]

As Warren Buffett noted:

It takes 20 years to build a reputation and five minutes to ruin it. If you think about that, you'll do things differently.

---

10 https://corporate.amp.com.au/newsroom/2019/may/amp-chairman_s-address-at-the-2019-annual-general-meeting

THE MENTOR PATHWAY

Another option you can consider at this stage in your career is that of mentoring, either formally or informally. We covered mentoring earlier in this book from the perspective of younger professionals seeking out mentors. At the other end of your executive career, mentoring is a highly productive, beneficial and satisfying role. Among other elements, mentoring younger people is a form of knowledge transfer that's hard to secure any other way. It also enables you to share your networks and help guide younger people through the options and pathways of their life and career. It's also about giving back, of recognising that there were people in your life who took the time to support you, so it's time to pay it back (and forward).

In addition, mentoring keeps you engaged and up to date with what's happening in your industry sector or profession and across the current and emerging national and global trends in business, trade, commerce, IoT, cyber security and more.

The options for mentoring are varied and range from professional business and leadership coaching organisations such as Stephenson Mansell and McCarthy Mentoring through to industry association mentoring programs or mentoring through the business or organisation you worked in.

You need to understand where your skills and networks are most relevant and useful and what you are passionate about and can add real value. For example, the Australian Institute of Company Directors has a specific directors' mentoring program for women. There are a number of organisations running mentoring programs for Aboriginal and Torres Strait Islanders, others for refugees wanting to start a business, the Asylum Seeker Resource Centre, Thrive

Refugee Enterprise and Settlement Services International to pick just three.[11]

Many state governments operate small business mentoring services that require business mentors and there's a wide range of start-up, scale-up and entrepreneurship mentoring opportunities, Catalysr, Startupbootcamp and Hunter Future Entrepreneurs among many others.[12]

Another excellent avenue for mentoring opportunities and engagement is through your university or tertiary education alumni networks. As an alumni of UTS, I am regularly involved in sharing my insights about branding and social enterprise with current students and alumni. While not a one-to-one experience, these presentations provide an avenue to share knowledge and be challenged by others.

RETIREMENT OR NOT

Of course, retirement is an option, and one many businesspeople are keen to take up as they are keen to work through their bucket list and enjoy life. The question of relevance across your key groups is still, well, highly relevant.

Just because you have time on your hands does not mean that others in your family, friend, business or community networks do. Your adult children are forging their own path and you're less relevant to them at this stage than even several years earlier. Your long-standing friends will probably have their own focus of attention, and it's

---

11 https://www.asrc.org.au/mentoring/, http://thriverefugeeenterprise.org.au/, https://www.ssi.org.au/

12 https://catalysr.com.au/, https://www.startupbootcamp.org/mentors/, https://www.hunterfuturepreneurs.com.au/mentors/

unlikely to be you. Similarly, your former colleagues may be in a different stage of their career or life, may still be working in a full-time or interim capacity, active on boards, involved with community organisations and so on.

Working out if and how you maintain your relevance across the different aspects of your life is critical at this point because unless you do you become irrelevant quite quickly. A former high-level executive recently shared with me that he stopped receiving phone calls after he'd stepped down from his reasonably high profile role. I asked him what he had done to ensure he was still engaged and active, and the response was 'nothing'. He thought that people would seek him out so he was waiting for the phone to ring – and it didn't.

'Brand you' is not where you work – it's who you are, what you stand for, your values and your expertise and knowledge. If you don't understand that, you're leaving yourself wide open to being defined by where you work, not who you are.

Good personal branding is hard. It requires self-awareness, action and accountability. You need to test it in your late 50s and 60s and assess if it's where you want it to be, and if it's not you have to work to change it, and it now requires a digital footprint. Glen Llopis, an expert in personal branding for leaders, notes that less than 15% of people have a truly defined personal brand and only 5% are living it consistently.[13] What he then shares is even more interesting.

> *70% of professionals **believe** they have defined their personal brand and 50% believe they are living it. But when you peel back the onion you realise that their focus was centred on*

13 https://www.forbes.com/sites/glennllopis/2013/04/08/personal-branding-is-a-leadership-requirement-not-a-self-promotion-campaign/#39df71ac226f

self-promotion rather than a commitment to advance themselves by serving others.

If you choose not to be engaged in some areas of your life, accept that means losing relevance and the ability to impact them.

In those areas that you want to maintain or build relevance, it's important to work on:

- how you define yourself
- how you reinvent or recalibrate what you are known for
- the way you present yourself
- how you engage
- your purpose and passion.

Doing nothing means you'll be on the escalator to the car park instead of the boardroom very quickly.

BRAND NEW DAD

Of course, your role as a parent changes at this time of your life. It is one of the greatest privileges and joys in life to become a parent, and also it brings significant responsibility and challenges.

When you first become a parent you recognise that it's life changing, however the enormity is only recognised in later years. Your whole positioning in life as an individual changes as it causes you to recalibrate your priorities and pursuits in life. Some people allocate their personal time, energy and talent differently when they become a parent, others don't.

There's a saying that the mark of good parenting is how your children turn out at the end! But the process is just as important and reflects to a significant degree how much time you have spent with your children throughout their lives at the different stages, and the ways you are relevant to them. I would like to think that I have – with my wife, Robyn – achieved success in both.

Being a father has had an even more profound impact on me in later life than being a CEO. Shepherding my sons through their various life stages and challenges has been a learning experience for me in itself, and I have used these experiences in my life both in and outside the family. It's certainly assisted me equally as much in my work as a mentor as my business experience.

I particularly like the quote by Mark Twain:

> *When I was a boy of 14, my father was so ignorant I could hardly stand to have the old man around. But when I got to be 21 I was astonished at how much the old man had learned in seven years.*

This, for me, also makes me reflect on my own father and how important fatherhood was to him. I started to think more about this later in my life as my sons were growing up.

Some final thoughts

Throughout *Brand New Brand You* I've endeavoured to follow the words of Harvard Business School professor Clay Christensen, who was asked to address a class of Harvard students in 2010. He related the story about meeting with the then Chairman of Intel, Andy Gove. Christensen had a very truncated amount of time to share some insights with Gove, so shared an analogy. It was afterwards he realised that 'instead of telling him what to think, I taught him how to think – and then he reached what I felt was the correct decision on his own.'[1]

I hope *Brand New Brand You* has given you a different way to think about you, your brand, reputation and purpose. It's up to you to explore what this means to you and to action, or not, the concepts and insights I've shared and to reflect on who you are, who you want to be, and your underlying purpose.

The effectiveness of 'brand you' is fundamentally about your relevance, as it's through your relevance that you can make an impact. Your relevance is about *what you can do*, not *who you are* – about being *something* not just *someone*.

1 'How Will You Measure Your Life?', Clay Christensen, *HBR*, July–August 2010.

At its most basic then relevance is simply having meaning or purpose, personally, professionally, or spiritually at a point in time.

To be *relevant*, you must be connected to a larger scheme, a grander plan. As leaders, we need to bring meaningful and purposeful solutions to the many perplexing issues in our world. The more relevant you are in whatever area you want to make an impact, the more impact you can make.

And your relevance changes over time and across different parts of your life.

Your reputation is equally important. It takes a lifetime to build and can be lost in a second.

Your purpose, underpinned by your values, however, is the most important component of 'brand you', and it's perhaps the one that's least explored. That's why I've spent a significant part of this book delving into it.

Deeply exploring your purpose and values will help guide the decisions you make and the strategy for your life.

To quote Christensen again:

> *Think about the metric by which your life will be judged and make a resolution to live every day so that in the end, your life will be judged a success.*[2]

2 Ibid.

ABOUT GARRY

Garry Browne AM has extensive CEO and Chair experience across business, not-for-profit, and education sectors, including the Foundation for National Parks and Wildlife, Life Education Australia, the Centre for Social Impact, Legacy, Rotary Foundation and UNSW International House. Garry is also Chairman of Stuart Alexander & Co, one of Australia's largest privately-owned companies, taking on this role after 20 years as CEO and Managing Director.

A highly respected business and industry leader, Garry has a proven record of introducing and building brands through traditional and non-traditional practices, expertise in transforming organisations, managing cultural change and leading innovative practices.

Garry collaborates with senior leaders, board members and communities across a range of organisations providing support, influence and leadership as well as mentoring younger up-and-coming leaders.

Contact Garry for keynote speaking, masterclasses, workshops, management and board development.

www.garrybrowne.com.au

ACKNOWLEDGEMENTS

I would like to acknowledge many friends, family, mentors, mentees and those who have shared their stories and wisdom with me along the way. You know who are.

Writing a book, as many know, doesn't just happen. It starts with an idea that evolves with a vision. Motivation helps to start that journey, and having experts around you makes an enormous difference. Much consultation is required with those who have done it before.

I have been so fortunate to be able to work with my good friend Jaqui Lane, who owns and runs The Book Adviser. Jaqui inspired me and gave me great advice in so many areas and topics, and helped me to capture the critical and important elements that allowed me to crystalise my thoughts and make this book a reality.

My friend John Green, author, publisher, company director and mentor, whose advice was most sound and pragmatic: 'There are two types of people who write books: those who start and those who finish.' I wanted to be in the latter group. John's advice inspired me to complete.

My friend, UTS Professor Simon Darcy, advised me on many occasions over a coffee not to undertake a PhD, which I was considering. His advice? 'Just go and write a book.'

Simon is an inspiration and an amazing human being.

My gratitude also goes to my publicist, Ro Markson of AC Agency, who has assisted me on a number of projects and encouraged me to really step out and promote this book.